P R A I S E   F O R

BLACKFACE

"In the past decade, African-American-inspired or produced films have gone from sporadic oddities to regular features of our cinematic landscape. Nelson George's behind-the-scenes look at the people and films that prompted this transformation is what makes his *Blackface: Reflections on African-Americans and the Movies* so fascinating."
—*Los Angeles Times*

"An essential look at the politics, problems and joys of black filmmaking."
—*Quarterly Black Review of Books*

"This is an exceptional book that serves as an outstanding companion to anyone interested in black films from the 1900s on through the present day . . . a must have book for any serious student of black film. An absolutely stunning work."   —*National Entertainment Plus Magazine*

"*Blackface* succeeds because it provides a little bit of something for everyone. Written in an exceedingly readable style . . . it is a treasure of personal observations and historical tidbits and belongs on the bookshelf of anyone interested in black cinema."   —*American-Statesman*

"Throughout, from his thoughts on the Poitier era and the emergence of the comic genius Richard Pryor to his gospel on the emergence of the Moses of black filmmaking, Spike Lee, George's odyssey proves fascinating, and often illuminating."   —*Hartford Courant*

"With the publication of *Blackface*, George has shown himself to be a formidable film cognoscente. It is a text that will definitely expand your knowledge of Black film history and sharpen your critical skills vis-à-vis the way in which you now access and interpret Black film."
—*Philadelphia Tribune*

"Potentially indispensable references and chronological devotion to the history of Blacks in film. Readers with an interest in popular culture will no doubt find the book i̇   ournal

Other Books by Nelson George

BLACKFACE

Reflections on

African-Americans

and the Movies

NELSON GEORGE

HarperPerennial

A Division of HarperCollins*Publishers*

A hardcover edition of this book was published in 1994 by HarperCollins Publishers.

BLACKFACE: REFLECTIONS ON AFRICAN-AMERICANS AND THE MOVIES. Copyright © 1994 by Nelson George. All rights reserved. Printed in the United States of America. No part of this book may be used or reproduced in any manner whatsoever without written permission except in the case of brief quotations embodied in critical articles and reviews. For information address HarperCollins Publishers, Inc., 10 East 53rd Street, New York, NY 10022.

HarperCollins books may be purchased for educational, business, or sales promotional use. For information please write: Special Markets Department, HarperCollins Publishers, Inc., 10 East 53rd Street, New York, NY 10022.

First HarperPerennial edition published 1995.

Designed by Nancy Singer

The Library of Congress has catalogued the hardcover edition as follows:

George, Nelson.
    Blackface : reflections on African-Americans and the movies / Nelson George. — 1st ed.
      p. cm.
    Includes index.
    ISBN 0-06-017120-0
    1. Afro-Americans in motion pictures. I. Title.
PN1995.9.N4G46 1994
791.43'6520396073—dc20   94-10686

ISBN 0-06-092658-9 (pbk.)

95 96 97 98 99 ❖/RRD 10 9 8 7 6 5 4 3 2 1

For my mother,
for all those Saturday afternoons
of movies and Chinese food

Contents

PROLOGUE

Hollywood

I sit outside the corner office of a top studio executive. A white business associate set up the meeting; he thought it would be good for the executive to talk with "an articulate black in touch with the street." In my mind I run through my rap about why African-American filmmakers and their audience should matter to Hollywood.

As I enter his office the film vet, younger than I expected, offers me an Evian and a place on his sofa. From his window there are bits of blue sky visible through the smog. He tells his secretary to hold his calls. I start talking. I hold his attention for, maybe, eighty seconds.

"Mind if I pace?" he inquires politely.

"No problem, man."

Thus begins a have-no-illusions diatribe that goes on for the rest of my half-hour. "We don't need specialists at this studio, Nelson," he opens, his body moving toward the door. "It's not about black film or knowing Spike or the Hudlin brothers. It's about who can bring in the idea for *Ninja Turtles II* or a series like *Friday the 13th*. Eventually we let people do a personal film, something they want to do," he says, strolling past me on his way toward the window.

I sip my Evian as he continues. "But first they have to make a couple of $100 million grossers. Studios let guys like Woody Allen and Spike Lee do what they do. It makes a little money or, at least, doesn't lose any. It generates good press. But, Nelson, we have a machine to feed."

Now he suddenly stands before me, not really intimidating, though it's strange to be suddenly looking him in the eye. "Theaters have to be filled. People have to be paid. So we've got to grind it out. We're in the pulp business." There was no evil in his voice. No malevolent chuckle. No irony either or undue concern. This is just the way it is. And, oh yeah, "Nice talking to you."

Canarsie

In the winter of 1991 I went over to my mother's house in East New York to pick up my two nieces, Ebony and Amber. They hadn't seen *Beauty and the Beast* yet and I was determined to be the one to take them. Ebony was ten and growing taller by the second. She's a voracious reader and TV viewer, but there was still a lot of baby in her. I always felt that Ebony was reluctant to get older, as if each year took her farther and farther from her preferred point in life. Amber, in contrast, was what folks used to call an old soul. She was five and small for her age. But there was a fierceness about her. She didn't mind a battle and would catch an attitude in a second. "No" was not a word she liked to hear in reponse to her stated desire. These two perfectly mismatched little girls were my only connection to childhood tastes, so I dearly wanted to see how they felt about Disney's latest.

We hopped a cab over to Canarsie, a once white, working-class neighborhood that by willpower blacks had finally integrated. It was one of those old neighborhood theaters that, along with drive-ins, were once the staples of American moviegoing. Red-cheeked white girls and a bored adult manager constituted the staff.

Inside the long, narrow theater (this was one of those single theaters reconstructed into a triplex) I slipped off the coats, balanced the popcorn, and made (what else) small talk with them. Ebony, a lover of sedentary activities, settled right in. Amber was happily restless. She wanted to sit where Ebony sat. She wanted to sit a row in front of us. She wanted the movie to start. She just wanted.

When it finally commenced, she quickly decided the Beast wasn't for her. "I want to go," she announced with conviction. I said, "No." She pouted. She demanded more soda. Then Ebony got into an argument with her, as siblings will do, and I thought I had a disaster in Canarsie underway. But then that Disney magic began to work. The score was captivating. The animation exceptional. Amber still didn't like the Beast, but she survived him before falling asleep in the final reel.

I don't know if Ebony and Amber will remember that night when they're fifteen, twenty-five, or thirty-five, but I really hope so. I hope it's one of those tidbits they'll recall one afternoon while stuck in traffic. And I hope it makes them smile and think well of their elderly old uncle. Going to the movies has always been one of my favorite things to do. My mother started my habit, and many of my best connections to moviegoing involve my mother and Andrea, Ebony and Amber's mother.

The book in your hand starts with those kinds of memories— memories most red-blooded Americans have of childhood. But my movie memories have grown more complicated and less comforting as I became involved, first in writing about movies, and then making them. Neither activity was premeditated. Writing about them was a total accident. Making them a matter of stumbling into a historic film and filmmaker.

But don't let me for a minute try to fool you: I'm a writer to my core. It's what sustains me; it gives my life meaning. So this work is not a celebration of me as a filmmaker or any particular work I've been involved with (an admittedly uneven bunch). The process is what intrigues me. How one goes from where Ebony and Amber sit, kids with popcorn watching a screen, to creating multimillion-dollar Hollywood-financed flicks is what this story attempts to explain. For those of you familiar with my previous pop culture histories, *The Death of Rhythm & Blues* and *Elevating the Game,* this text is something of a departure. Although there is quite a bit of history covered in *Blackface,* this book leans as much on my own experiences as analyses of others' accomplishments.

Blackface is more a memoir than a critique. In covering music I was a critic and a fan, in basketball an amateur jock but mostly observer; in film I've been a cheerleader, consumer, and professional participant, so my relationship to the story I'm telling here is very different. I'm not so much driving toward a grand theory of the black image in film as expanding on my journey in hopes that the particulars of my experience will strike a chord. Think of it as a book with the open-ended quality of a Spike Lee script but lacking Ernest Dickerson's cinematography; you'll just have to trust me to make this narrative's images vivid.

Blackface's throughline (one of those clever terms I learned in Hollywood) is the viewing experience. From childhood to this day I've loved going to theaters to see movies, and I've always been fascinated by the chemistry between the movie and moviegoers, strangers united by their appearance in a place—a private screening room, a sedate cinema, a narrow multiplex, an ancient old-style motion picture palace—to see light bounce back off a screen and into their eyes. Watching home videos or high-quality laser discs is all well and good. But that strange magic, that slipping into a collective dream a good film makes possible, forms the spine of *Blackface*.

I chose *Blackface* as my title for several reasons. It's a word that resonates with the (mis)use of African-American artists and their image, which is one thread of this narrative. It also suggests to me the complicated journey African-Americans go on in search of images of themselves and our complicated reponses to what we find. White and black performers in the early part of this century wore burnt cork makeup, emblematic of putting on a face of pseudo-blackness. Wearing that cork mask meant the performers spoke, sang, moved, and joked within a highly coded and stylized mode of "black" (aka "colored" or "negro") behavior.

Though the burnt cork mask is now part of history, my four decades of active moviegoing have presented similarly "corrected" images of black behavior. Sidney Poitier, Ron O'Neal, Diana Ross, Eddie Murphy, and Ice Cube have all, in their different ways, worn their "blackfaces" to present (and define) who we, African-Americans, were. There can be no dispute that contemporary black filmmakers have brought more nuance to the African-American image. Yet within the ranks of these folks, arguments rage in seminars, reviews, interviews, and, most vividly, in the images they create about which blackface is the right "blackface."

Although *Blackface* isn't intended as a "history" of African-Americans in film, my critical heart still beats. I couldn't resist getting my two cents in about the range of black participation in American movies during my moviegoing lifetime. So intercut between this book's chapters is a black film timeline that puts my more anecdotal material in perspective.

I decided to start the timeline with Sidney Poitier's ascension to superstardom with his Academy Award win as best actor in *Lilies of the Field*. The acceptance of a black dramatic star, coming as it did during the height of the civil rights movement, was of historic importance in and out of the industry. Moreover, if you trace

Poitier's development from star to producer-director, you get a pointed view of the evolution of black filmmakers within Hollywood. Almost everything that the current crop of African-American filmmakers and actors have tried within the system was accomplished or attempted by Poitier first.

In fact much of what's happened in black film since Poitier's glory days can be seen as either a reaction to or critique of his work. Staunchly integrationist and a figure of old school dignity, Poitier has cast a shadow that still lingers. No black actor or actress since has combined the high critical respect and consistent commercial appeal he possessed in the sixties. Despite the protest of many black observers at the time, Poitier's presence in a film, no matter the subject matter or approach, gave it a black credibility to whites and a great many blacks. Today this issue is still relevant, since the appearance of a Whoopi Goldberg or Wesley Snipes in a film, no matter who directs or scripts, raises the same question of blackness today. I also have special affection for the man's body of work, which makes it a pleasure to highlight him.

My criteria for inclusion in this timeline was that an entry had to be a theatrical film or some fact related to theatrical films. There are a few exceptions made for certain television shows, commercials, or music videos, but not many. The success of an actor, a style or theme in television, for example, did not always translate into a movie career. Moreover, the process by which television programs are funded, produced, and distributed is, even today, so radically different that it would be like mixing apples and celery to blend them together here. The chance for a wild-card project to break through in film is infinitely greater than on American television, whether it be network, public, or even cable.

In the thirty-year period covered here, not every black-controlled or -themed film is listed—remember, this is an intentionally subjective guide, not an absolute history—though I hope it serves to give a panoramic picture of the years covered. Several projects I've been involved with are mentioned in the timeline, though the gory personal details are saved for the body of the text.

As I put this timeline together, several trends became apparent. From 1963 to 1971 Sidney Poitier was far and away the preeminent African-American figure in film, while a few of his black Hollywood peers (Sammy Davis, Jr., Harry Belafonte) fashioned individual star vehicles. For the most part it was white independent filmmakers who were able to raise the capital to present nonmainstream views of African-Americans. At the end of this cycle Jim Brown emerged as the first black macho man of Hollywood and served as a bridge between Poitier's assimilated characters and the ghettocentric protagonists to come. The years 1971 to 1974 were defined by the stud sons and badass daughters of *Sweetback*. It was an epoch foreshadowed by Ossie Davis's *Cotton Comes to Harlem*, but truly energized by Melvin Van Peebles's innovative film, which was quickly formularized into either cool supercops (*Shaft*, *Slaughter*) or criminal antiheroes (*Superfly*, *The Mack*).

Not as well noted by critics or, unfortunately, audiences were a surprisingly steady flow of nonblaxploitation features that started in 1972 and ended in 1978 with the $30 million flop of Universal's *The Wiz*. In many cases poor distribution and publicity or botched execution made them commercial and/or artistic failures. Many were based on plays, autobiographies, or novels, often by black authors. Films that fit this category include *Georgia, Georgia*, *The River Niger*, *Black Girl*, and *The Greatest*. The biggest successes of this sub-genre were *Sounder*, *Cooley High*, and *Claudine*. Sad to say, at this point in the current wave of black film there have yet to be made three nonghettocentric films of equivalent quality and popularity.

In the mid-seventies black independent films began building a critical following through showings on college campuses, at museums, and at film festivals in both the United States and Europe. Most of this work was financed by local and federal government grants, charitable foundations, or the filmmakers themselves. Charles Burnett's *Killer of Sheep*, completed in 1977, is generally regarded as the best black indie film of the decade and the most enduring of the many black indie projects to emerge from Los Angeles during this era.

The years from 1977 to 1982 belonged, in the public mind, to Richard Pryor. The rebellious, troubled comic became America's biggest black star since Poitier, though Hollywood (and Pryor himself) consistently wasted his unique talent. Away from the hype of Hollywood, the founding of the Black Filmmaker Foundation in

New York gave black indie film a platform in the nation's media capital.

Eddie Murphy, right after reviving NBC's "Saturday Night Live," exploded onto the big screen with a string of funny, charismatic performances that made 1982 to 1987 the peak of his Hollywood reign. His cockiness was a real departure from Pryor's insecure, nervous style. Again, away from the bright lights, a number of film school graduates and frustrated actors were writing and shooting indie projects.

From 1986 through 1990 they made their commercial breakthrough with Spike Lee serving as the point man. The presence of an opinionated, gifted, visionary African-American auteur energized audiences and set the stage for peers Robert Townsend, Keenen Ivory Wayans, and Reggie and Warrington Hudlin.

The twelve months of 1991 go down as the biggest year in Hollywood history for black directors. There were commercial and critical triumphs. There were profound failures. Audience support of the harder-edged material and rejection of both period films and class-based comedies was a crucial trend that currently still affects Hollywood financing decisions. Since then the black film scene has been dominated by two very different big-budget films, Spike Lee's *Malcolm X* and Reggie Hudlin's Eddie Murphy vehicle, *Boomerang*. Two very different features directed by black women, Julie Dash's *Daughters of the Dust* and Leslie Harris's *Just Another Girl on the I.R.T.*, reached art houses. A number of directors made their second and third features, but it was stars like Wesley Snipes, Whoopi Goldberg and, in a big surprise, Whitney Houston, who emerged with crossover power.

I won't know if seeing *Beauty and the Beast* was at all important to my nieces for quite a while. But it was to me, even if only because the ultimate result is still in doubt. That's the thing about movies— you never know what they'll finally mean to your psyche or your soul. All I know for sure is that when you open your eyes something enters you. So often for me it's been a black face.

P.S. The Black Filmmaker Foundation newsletter, also known as *Blackface*, influenced my title choice.

Part One

WATCHING MOVIES
1963–1969

T I M E L I N E

1963

Sidney Poitier gives an Academy Award–winning performance as Homer Smith in *Lilies of the Field*. As a drifter who aids a bunch of stubborn nuns in fixing their church, Poitier was warm, funny, and conciliatory toward whites. By making these white women nuns, the question of his sexuality was muted, while brotherhood across the racial divide was celebrated. His win anointed him the first black male film star of the civil rights era and made this thirty-six-year-old actor the artistic guardian of the "positive" black image for the next ten years.

Sidney Poitier, a role model's role model. (Courtesy of *New York Daily News*.)

Shirley Clarke's *The Cool World*, an indie film with a screenplay co-written by Carl Lee (later to play Eddie in *Superfly*), is shot on location in Harlem. In a gritty documentary style this white filmmaker paints a harsh, yet sympathetic story of a teenaged Harlem street gang named Duke. It's an edgy coming-of-age film that in atmosphere, though not action, and tone anticipates the ghettocentric cinema of the nineties.

Gone Are the Days is adapted by Ossie Davis from his play about race relations, *Purlie Victorious*, and is co-produced by Brock Peters. Davis stars along with Ruby Dee and Godfrey Cambridge. Though Davis didn't direct, the movie began the actor's long involvement with roles behind the camera. This piece will have a later life as a Broadway musical, *Purlie*, starring Melba Moore and Cleavon Little.

Cleveland Browns football star Jim Brown (considered the greatest running back in National Football League history) is paid $37,000 to appear in *Rio Conchos*.

1964

German-born filmmaker Michael Roemer shoots one of the greatest black experience films of all time. *Nothing But a Man*, with Ivan Dixon, Abbey Lincoln, Gloria Foster, and the young Yaphet Kotto, is a wonderfully nuanced look at the marriage of a working-class brother and the daughter of a minister in Mississippi. Domestic tension, economic roadblocks, racism, and the characters' basic humanity are all well balanced in this understated production.

Ralph Ellison publishes a perceptive essay on Hollywood's socially conscious "problem" films of the fifties (the problem being black folks) in his collection of essays, *The Shadow and the Act*.

1965

Actress Dorothy Dandridge dies in Los Angeles at forty-two. The bronze beauty had been nominated for the best actress Oscar for her sultry performance in 1954's *Carmen Jones*. Her life was as tragic as her on-screen persona was luminous and haunting.

Jim Brown retires from the Cleveland Browns when training camp conflicts with the filming of *The Dirty Dozen* in England. His death scene is one of the first truly exciting action sequences involving a black star. He goes on to make eleven films between 1967 and 1970.

The Pawnbroker, Sidney Lumet's directorial debut, features jazz-flavored compositions by Quincy Jones. It is the arranger-trumpeter's first score and the beginning of a long career in Hollywood.

A lot of black people never forgave Poitier for his work in *A Patch of Blue*, a silly unrequited love story between Poitier and a blind white girl. At times Poitier's character seemed embarrassed to admit he was "Negro" to the girl.

Senegalese novelist-turned-director Ousmane Sembène is the first sub-Saharan filmmaker to have a film debuted at the Cannes Film Festival. His *Black Girl* tells the sad tale of Diouana, a Senegalese au pair who travels to France with the family she works for. Speaking no French and kept in the family's home as a virtual slave, Diouana's life eventually ends in tragedy. As a metaphor for the relationship between Africa and its colonizing countries, *Black Girl* was a biting work of criticism that announced Sembène's artistry to the world.

Gillo Pontecorvo's *The Battle of Algiers* is a masterpiece of anti-imperialist propaganda that shows the successful struggle of an African people against a European colonial power, aka the French. The third world's great revolutionary thinker Frantz Fanon is an inspiration for much of Pontecorvo's approach. The image of grenades hidden in the robes of Muslim women not only showed how the Algerians threw off the French, but was a harbinger of how first versus third world struggles would be fought around the globe.

1966

A Man Called Adam is a Sammy Davis Jr. vehicle in which the multitalented entertainer plays a rather unconvincing jazz musician. There is much capable support in Louis Armstrong, Ossie Davis, Lola Falana, and rat-pack partner Peter Lawford. However, Davis is too mannered to capture the destructive charm of the character. The destructive black jazz musician, a staple stereotype of hip culture, wouldn't be properly depicted until saxophonist Dexter Gordon's work in *Round Midnight* twenty years later.

LeRoi Jones's searing play *Dutchman* is adapted into a short film starring Al Freeman, Jr.

1967

■ Sidney Poitier's three films, *To Sir with Love*, *In the Heat of the Night*, and *Guess Who's Coming to Dinner*, make him the number one box-office star in America.

■ According to *Variety*, blacks constitute 15 percent of the U.S. population and 30 percent of the moviegoing audience. "The black population of this country comprises a much larger proportion of the motion-picture audience than its proportion of our total population would indicate," says *Variety*.

■ *The Comedians*, a big-budget adaptation of Graham Greene's bestseller about modern Haiti stars Elizabeth Taylor and Richard Burton, but features vibrant supporting performances by James Earl Jones, Raymond St. Jacques, and Roscoe Lee Browne.

■ Melvin Van Peebles directs the interracial romance *The Story of a Three-Day Pass* in Paris. The film, made for $100,000, was celebrated at the San Francisco Film Festival. It was, ironically, the official French entry. Its acclaim landed Van Peebles a deal with Columbia Pictures.

1968

■ *Still a Brother*, an award-winning documentary by Williams Greaves and William Branch about the black middle class, focuses on a group usually missing from American film, yet so crucial to the civil rights movement.

■ Sidney Poitier and Abbey Lincoln star in the black love story *For Love of Ivy*, developed from Poitier's idea.

■ In one of the first black-white buddy action films Sammy Davis Jr. and Peter Lawford co-headline *Salt and Pepper*. This lightweight James Bond—like film spawns a 1970 sequel, *One More Time*. They walk through the film as if they were as cute as they think they are.

■ *If He Hollers, Let Him Go*, starring Raymond St. Jacques and Barbara McNair, is based loosely on a Chester Himes novel and is noteworthy for its steamy sex scene between St. Jacques and the singer McNair. Many found St. Jacques a refreshing contrast to the relatively chaste Poitier.

- Jules Dassin's *Up Tight*, adapted from the John Ford film *The Informer*, stars Raymond St. Jacques, Julian Mayfield, and Ruby Dee. Ruby Dee and Mayfield co-scripted this rather incoherent look at infighting among black revolutionaries in Cleveland.

- *The Scalphunters*, an entertaining B movie, features a long, brutal fight scene between Ossie Davis and Burt Lancaster that doesn't end with the white man victorious.

- George Romero's *Night of the Living Dead*, one of the most influential of the low-budget midnight horror films to proliferate in the seventies, has a black actor, Duane Jones, as its protagonist. Like Poitier and St. Jacques, Jones projects an urbane, upwardly mobile attitude in his idealized role as the ever resourceful black survivor. In every one of the *Living Dead* sequels a black character would play either the lead or a prominent supporting role.

1969

- Photographer Gordon Parks Sr. makes his directing debut with an adaptation of his autobiography, *The Learning Tree*. Though little remembered today, this moving story of a young black boy growing up in Kansas in the twenties has all the elements of sensitivity, insight, and class that black audiences have always craved.

- *Putney Swope* is a farce about blacks taking over a Madison Avenue ad agency. Despite its scattershot comedy there's a cynicism about the changes blacks could make by simply moving up the corporate ladder that resonates.

- Jim Brown is paid $200,000 to appear in *100 Rifles* with Raquel Welch.

A THEATER IN BROWNSVILLE

I grew up in a Jewish neighborhood that I watched turn black. Pitkin Avenue in Brownsville was a thriving commercial shopping strip that had been created by the Jewish merchants whose families once also populated its streets. In the early sixties, many of the stores still had Jewish names, while the more generic businesses (Thom McAn's, Woolworth's, East New York Savings Bank) were still largely staffed by folks with Jewish surnames.

As I grew older Brownsville became blacker and blacker, and more brown faces stared back at me from behind the counter. Ominously stores began to disappear. Either unwilling or unable to sell to blacks, Puerto Ricans, or Arabs, many Jewish store owners shut them down (or burned them), leaving holes on Pitkin that urban renewal never replaced. You couldn't totally blame the merchants. Crime rose, not with the arrival of blacks, but with the influx of heroin. My mother was always wary of purse snatching, so I know the shopkeepers were uptight about shoplifting, much less armed robberies. These were the years when rioting and revolution were thought interchangeable, and the phrase "rip off" entered the vocabulary. Fear drove them away.

So did ghosts from their past. The Brownsville they'd known that had nurtured their people and their businesses had by the late sixties largely disappeared. Their old clients had split for Canarsie or Long Island or Florida, fleeing my family and my friends as if we were a deadly dark plague. Whatever bond the Jews and blacks enjoyed during the civil rights movement, in the city's political clubs and in the NAACP, meant nothing on Pitkin where Semite merchant met black customer. I recall some kind men and women overwhelmed by a suspicion and fear I felt but didn't yet understand.

At the far west end of Pitkin, a block or two before the avenue melted into Eastern Parkway, was the Olympic Theater. To get there from the Tilden Projects (where I lived with my mother and sister) you could take a bus from Livonia Avenue under the elevated subway station up Rockaway Avenue past the Brownsville projects, a church, cheap furniture stores, the Belmont Avenue strip (best known for its fish market), and up to Pitkin. Once there, you got a transfer and rode the ten or so blocks to the theater. Of course, if you were like me you tried to hold on to every dime (they could be scarce) and walked the many blocks to movie heaven.

Along the way you bought cherry ices, ogled the latest sneakers, and kept your eye open for cats looking to cop your movie money. Even in the days before angel dust and crack, it was safer to travel Brownsville's streets posse deep. I must admit, however, that the biggest threat to my Saturdays was my own forgetfulness. On the way to the theater I lost along Pitkin Avenue glasses, baseball caps, watches, jackets, and enough dimes, quarters, and dollars to finance my college education. Between skeptical merchants, the odd young mugger, and my unnatural clumsiness, each journey to Pitkin and the theater held forth the possibility of adventure.

Which was fine since the theater itself went from nondescript to downright horrible. It was a big, old ornate movie palace whose lineage went back to vaudeville and certainly smelled like it. As a symbol of Pitkin's decay the smell of the venerable old theater lingers. First it was just mildew in the restrooms. As the theater evolved from a cross-cultural meeting place into a Saturday ritual playground for burgeoning numbers of black and Puerto Rican children, the smell spread. With time the scarlet carpet turned crimson with ground-in dirt. Broken seats proliferated. Ticket prices rose. But most vivid to me is that smell, that smell that said management didn't care, the smell that said we weren't as important as the customers who'd come before.

I remember clearly two movies I saw at that theater. In 1964, Paramount Studios released *Zulu*, a celebration of British imperialism whose set piece depicted a gallant regiment of redcoats trapped in a crumbling compound as a mad tribe of Zulu attacked and attacked and attacked. The good old boys from Merseyside were valorous and died in gritty close-ups. They lined up on disciplined lines. They fired, reloaded, and fired into the waves of brown- and black-skinned Zulus who, in broad daylight, served themselves up as cannon fodder. Except for close-ups of the scowling Zulu chieftain, a character undoubtedly based on Shaka, the Zulu king, the Africans were photographed in a distant, impersonal manner. They were bodies where the soldiers were faces.

As a black child (or a child of any color, for that matter), you wanted to root for the folks who looked like you. But the film's visual strategy left little room for anything but the mildest racial identification. Leaving the afternoon matinee you best believe the kids were not imitating the Zulu's tactic of running headlong into gunfire, but those redcoated Brits pulling triggers under a bloody sun. Though blue was my favorite color, I remember getting a red baseball cap at the time just so I could connect with the heroism of that valiant company. After all, the Zulu may have been brown-skinned, but they were African and I was still a Negro.

Or was I a monkey? Negro or monkey seemed to me the options presented by *Planet of the Apes*, the other flick I remember seeing on one of those classic summer Saturdays. I rolled into the theater with two friends. We planted ourselves in the back row, popcorn piled as high as we could afford, and watched Charlton Heston, truly the white man's white man, try to make sense of a world where the master race were slaves and monkeys were running things.

Since a typical insult of my childhood was "You monkey-faced fool!" or, more pointedly, "You monkey-faced motherfucker!" the idea of a world conquered by primates who treated whitey like crap raised a number of interesting issues. If you accepted being called a monkey, should *Planet of the Apes* be viewed as vindication? If you didn't accept being called a monkey and remained a Negro, did that mean you didn't exist anymore since Negroes were scarce in the film (a black astronaut arrived from the past with Heston, but was quickly stuffed and mounted by the apes as an artifact of a bygone era). If you identified with the apes, because your nose or forehead too closely matched that of one of the lead-ape actors, did that mean you agreed with the brutality directed toward whites? On an even more personal—and scary—level, if you identified with the apes did you dare tell any of your friends?

Between popcorn bites and listening to monkey insults shouted across the theater, I wrestled inconclusively with these questions as Charlton Heston planned his escape. A man of granite jaw and equally granite expressions, Heston and his grimacing countenance apparently had a heroic appeal for mainstream America that escaped Pitkin's audience. A lot of folks in the theater were rooting for the apes to lobotomize him. Many were more happy than shocked when, at the film's end, a fractured Statue of Liberty was seen stuck in the sand to Heston's horror.

There was a general "That's what fools deserve" feeling in the theater. Maybe if there was some sense that black folks were still alive in the future, my peers would have cut Heston more slack. But unlike the politically correct sci-fi of the nineties, issues of black inclusion weren't on Hollywood's mind back in 1968.

In retrospect the really funny thing was that Heston, Mr. Aryan neocon stud, who'd played that most Jewish of Jews Moses, was the last real white man left. I'm sure that wasn't lost on the filmmakers and publicity flacks. These subtleties were lost on me then. All I knew for sure was that Heston didn't look like any of the Jewish merchants left on Pitkin Avenue.

ACTING COOL

One of the most resonant experiences of my moviegoing child-hood occurred on Flatbush Avenue in 1964 when my mother took me to see Alfred Hitchcock's *Marnie*. It was my first sighting of Sean Connery (I had been too young to see *Dr. No*; *Goldfinger* would be my first James Bond film). *Marnie* was a psychosexual thriller (Hitchcock didn't really make any other kind) that starred Tippi Hedren as the director's trademark icy blond and the rugged, perfectly cast Connery as the sexy white boy. For me the film's key moment occurred when Hedren and Connery confronted each other in a bedroom—he in a robe and she in just a white towel. She slapped him for an insolent crack; he slapped her back with a quickness. Hitchcock cut from her face to the floor, where the towel fell to her feet, back to his face. Always maintaining his cool, Connery nevertheless projected a lust I'd never seen on screen before. At that time I had no idea what a naked woman's body looked like, but the juxtaposition of anger, nudity, and passion in the editing stirred me. Love was not in Connery's eyes, but there was a yearning, a will to dominate and caress, that made me very uncomfortable to be sitting next to my mom. Well into my teens, Connery remained something of a sexual role model for me. While no one moment in any Bond flick was as psychologically complex as that confrontation in *Marnie*, 007's sexual conquests allowed me to feel potent by sharing in his voracious appetites. As a bookworm, I also had the distinct pleasure of reading Ian Fleming's Bond books and marking the "dirty" parts for repeat inspections, while my friends had only the impermanence of film to recall.

Connery projected (and still projects) a cocky, I'm-in-total-control cool that I'd rarely seen in white men. He proved that cool wasn't limited to black men (though my boys countered that whites only had it in Hollywood). Bond only made sense to me then as a white boy who'd spent a lot of time hanging with bloods. None of the white kids I went to school with were anywhere near as cool as Connery. Nor did their parents or my teachers possess the neces-sary command.

There was, however, one assistant principal at P.S. 189 with flavor. Let's call him Mr. Feldman. He was lean with dark hair, wore well-tailored gray suits, owned a sports car, and was always whispering to some young student teacher in the hallway. He was as close as I got to encountering a possibly cool white guy. Still, he worked at an elementary school, and no matter how many college girls he pulled, you couldn't hang with Bond if the only mystery in your life was running down truants.

The black men I knew who could hang with Connery were friends of my mother's who called themselves the Afrodisiacs III. The Afrodisiacs gave parties in Brooklyn and in the then new black homeowning area, Jamaica, Queens. Two were unforgettable. Gary was well built and lanky with a large round head and wide, droopy eyes. He laughed often, but with a reserve that never let him seem out of control—control being as crucial to cool as diamond bracelets are to Tiffany's windows. Gary is immortal to me because he was the first person I knew to own a Mustang back when that was the Aston Martin of the ghetto—sleek, fast, and definitely outta sight. When Gary used to pull his Mustang up outside the projects and take my sister and me to Coney Island for Wonder Wheel rides and Nathan's shrimp, I felt I shared some of his power.

As groovy as Gary was, though, my main man, the sepia Bond of my world, the truest example of cool at its most profound, was Eddie, known to all his friends as E.M. E.M. was the first non-teacher I knew who made his living wearing a suit. My man was an insurance claims investigator. An investigator! Sporting dark green shades, a mohair suit, a narrow tie, a white shirt, shiny shoes, and an attaché case, E.M. looked good every day. No visible sweat glands. Inside his attaché case was a Polaroid camera with ice-cube bulbs that were great to play with (and break). Coolest of all, E.M. had a Volkswagen when that was a very avant-garde move for a brother.

But beyond the threads and the gig, E.M. was just cool. Whatever set of physiological, psychological, and environmental factors manifests itself in a persona that's relaxed, unstressed, yet never at rest, well, E.M. had it. And he had the beautiful companions who come with that quality. Most of his women were honey brown with brown or auburn hair—I well remember Shirley, a curvy, loud lady with a taste for reddish-orange wigs. But I adored Charley, a smallish woman with an impish humor who always wore halter tops and used to give me great big hugs that drove my adolescent hormones crazy. E.M. was cool and Charley was bubbly. Watching them together made me real anxious to grow up.

Aside from his busy job and his active love life, E.M. somehow managed to raise three daughters. When he and his wife split up, E.M. kept the girls, wisely moving into the same development as his parents, who provided much needed backup. My mother reminds me that much of E.M.'s appeal was his ability to juggle his sundry responsibilities with so few signs of strain. E.M. was such an over-whelming presence that it wasn't until my teens that I began to peep into the dark side of his cool world. My first inkling came one Sunday afternoon when he stopped by to watch Joe Namath's Jets take on the Colts during one of Johnny Unitas's last Baltimore campaigns. Bombs were flying all day as the two great quarterbacks dueled for bragging rights. But from behind his shades E.M. gave me little feedback. In retrospect I know he was as high as a kite, though I don't know on what; then I just figured my James Bond was tired. Not too long after that, the facade finally collapsed. Among E.M.'s many recreational activities was weekend hunting. He had the bad habit of dumping his rifles in his bedroom dresser. One evening he and Charley, apparently quite high, began playing with one of the guns. It went off. Charley died of the wound. E.M. was indicted for manslaughter. When he got out years later, he wasn't so much cool as subdued. He devoted his life to counseling kids in Harlem, trying to help them find their way past cool, before dying of lung cancer in 1990.

Robert Farris Thompson writes that in the African Yoruba language, "Coolness, then, is part of character, and character objectifies proper custom. To the degree that we live generously and discreetly, exhibiting grace under pressure, our appearance and our acts gradually assume virtual royal power." At his best E.M. was regal—at least he seemed so to a single-parent kid looking for real-life heroes. Cool obviously masked the conflicts E.M.'s pioneering white-collar job, responsibilities as a father, and nocturnal spirit brought with them. But it couldn't protect him forever. Cool, while infinitely attractive, seems more effective as an acting style than a lifestyle choice. And even in that context there are very few Sean Connerys.

SIDNEY & ME

When I was twenty-one I bought a book titled *The Films of Sidney Poitier*. In format it was no different from others I'd seen about Anthony Quinn, Edward G. Robinson, and Robert Mitchum. Plenty of publicity stills, synopses of each flick, samples from representative reviews, and cast and crew credits. It was strictly for hard-core fans of the actor. It wasn't art, but it was the first book I'd ever seen about a black actor and I bought it immediately.

But then being the first black man to do this or that was one of the burdens of Sidney's life. No other black actor, and few black figures, was so massive a figure in our (in this case American) psyche. No one else has meant what he did and no one else ever will, though it's grand to see Denzel Washington, Wesley Snipes, Morgan Freeman, etc., all trying.

Leafing through that book now is, just as it was back in 1978, like a Rorschach test for me. All these memories of who I was, what I wanted to be, and sundry misjudgments along the way leap back into my head. The book's introductory essay stated that Poitier, though born in Miami, was reared in the Bahamas and arrived in New York in 1943 with nothing but a thick accent and great ambition. I'd never known Sidney was what we ignorantly called West Indian when I'd first seen his work and, very likely, it would have negatively affected my view of him. Before Bob Marley and ganja and Rastafarianism put an Afrocentric, rootsy spin on the American view of Caribbean culture, I'd always viewed its transplanted natives as snobby, snotty, and uppity, based on my own experiences.

An upper-crust merchant class had been settled in Brooklyn for years. They had houses, first in Bedford-Stuyvesant and Crown Heights, and later in Flatlands, East Flatbush, and Flatbush proper. I went to school with their kids. I visited their neat little homes. I felt the odd condescending tone in an adult voice. I sensed they felt it was a shame I lived in the projects and my parents were from "down South," not from Trinidad, Barbados, or Jamaica. Who were these funny-talking fools to disrespect us? I don't remember any fistfights over the matter, but there was a real tension between us and them, skin color be damned.

But Sidney, whose career was built on masquerading as an

African-American, successfully avoided our prejudices. The very qualities I admired in Sidney were the things that made me resent the West Indians that I knew. The irony is that a lot of the regal bearing he projected could, in another context, have been seen as insufferable superiority. The most sympathetic thing about Rod Steiger's redneck sheriff in *In the Heat of the Night* was that the poor guy had to grapple with Sir Sid at his most lordly. It's one of Sidney's few parts where he let his class consciousness overwhelm his charm and, as a result, it's one of his deepest characterizations. Just as I went to Sidney's movies to escape the unstable ghetto around me, his career was very much his aping of the bearing of the Caribbean bourgeois. That he rose to prominence playing doctors, lawyers, detectives—protobuppies all—is a logical extension of his own rise from poverty on an obscure little island.

Though the book is arranged chronologically, my own understanding of Sidney's career works in reverse. I learned about his early films, the ones in which he fought his way up the Hollywood food chain, only after being seduced by the established icon. I was ten in 1967 and I saw all three of the flicks that made him America's number one box office draw. *In the Heat of the Night*, *To Sir with Love*, and *Guess Who's Coming to Dinner* were the high points of his career commercially, the peak from which he would begin, artistically and socially, to slide gradually into a self-imposed exile as a dramatic actor. Not incidental to experiencing these films was that my mother and sister went with me to see them.

In *To Sir with Love* he played Mark Thackeray, a teacher from British Guiana (one of his rare portrayals as a Caribbean native) who converts a classroom of cockney kids into respectable British citizens. At the time my mother was going to Brooklyn College in search of a degree in education and working as a paraprofessional in a Brownsville school. The notion of turning around all the students in a renegade class in one semester thus was pretty farfetched to us, but still the film resonated for us. The struggle to connect with unruly students, to integrate yourself into a hostile bureaucratic environment, and the daily fear of failure—failure to reach kids who desperately need what you know but won't acknowledge that fact—were things my mother told me or I overheard her discuss with her friends.

While Sidney's color played an unrealistically small part in the students' reaction to Thackeray, the very fact of his blackness led my family into a kinship with his teacher. I definitely got a little misty-eyed myself when Lulu serenaded Sidney with "To Sir with Love," though when he danced with one of the white students we had to laugh. He had the dignity part cold but his rhythm was way off. In *To Sir* Sidney had little backup. He had a rookie director, no other stars, and had to sell a nonperiod British story to xenophobic Americans. Yet he made it work.

In the Heat of the Night was a very different piece. The Canadian Norman Jewison was a world-class director, Rod Steiger a scene-chewing actor, and its plot of a black Northern detective solving a murder in a Mississippi town was a fish-out-of-water story years before it became a screenwriter's cliché.

This was the film that really made me fall for Sidney. Even in the wilting southern heat the second button on his suit always stayed closed. Anger flashed across his face when he slapped a racist southern patriarch and shouted at Steiger's sheriff, "I'm a police officer!" But flash was all it did. He never seemed consumed by it or, more important, let white folks know how deeply his anger burned. For his cops, Virgil Tibbs's competence was his weapon. His quiet class expressed his contempt for the slovenly white world that he moved in and that distrusted him. Again, as in *Sir*, it's Sidney's basic decency that awakens all the white folks around him to their own moral failures. Surely, outside Dr. King, no other Negroes walked the earth with Sidney's forbearance and wisdom.

As inhumanly unrealistic as Tibbs was, Sidney made him work. And by breathing life into such a creature, Sidney breathed Tibbs into me. James Bond might conquer the women. The charismatic young politician Julian Bond sparkled on my TV. Willie Mays was still roaming the San Francisco outfield. But Sidney's heroic bearing, that face full of character and intelligence and confidence, made him the man I wanted to be. Today I know I've failed in my efforts to replicate Sir Sid. In 1967, however, it all seemed possible. If he existed, so could I.

The dark side of this film was how disconnected Sidney's Tibbs was from the black community. Only Beah Richards as Mama Caleba, the local abortionist, had a real role among the supporting black cast. In real life a big-city black detective in a Mississippi town would have received tons of support from its black citizens. A lot of his time would have been spent fielding dinner invitations from single church women and their eager families. He'd have been on the cover of the local black paper. He'd have been given a room at the local black hotel or stayed with the local black undertaker or general store owner on the dark side of town. Some would have praised him, holding Tibbs up (as the real world did Sidney) as a role model for the race. Others would have thought his manner stiff and diction difficult to understand. A nasty few would have thought him an Uncle Tom. And what of white women? The widow of the murdered industrialist and the slutty girl whose lover turns out to be the murderer both recklessly eyeball Tibbs. Would there not have been some seriously impressed white lass who would have made a move on this unique color flavor?

That question is, of course, the starting point of *Guess Who's Coming to Dinner?* As another black Superman, Dr. John Prentice, Sidney woos and wins the young heiress to a newspaper baron's fortune before the opening credits. Of course the deep wells of fantasy and lust that would underpin this union have no place in Stanley Kramer's dull, polite feature. Even as a starstruck kid I knew *Dinner* was too chaste by far. The word "pussy" had already been added to my vocabulary. I'd read it written on the concrete playground. I'd heard it spoken by teenagers and a few bold kids my age. The sexlessness that Sidney got so criticized for hit me in *Dinner*. His fiancée, the comely Katharine Houghton, deserved more than some light lip rubbing in the back of a taxi.

The film was really about liberal guilt, anyway. It was about those icons of sexual fantasy, Spencer Tracy and Katharine Hepburn, coming to terms with their daughter's acting on the platitudes they'd so often spoken. Like most of Stanley Kramer's work it was as high-minded, liberal, and boring as George McGovern in '72.

Other than that *Guess* made little impression on me despite its risqué subject matter. Much more memorable and fun was *For Love of Ivy*, a little-remembered film that was his 1968 follow-up to his hit-making '67 trilogy. It was a love story that Poitier conceived about a slick gambler blackmailed into dating a black maid played by the lovely Abbey Lincoln. I guess this was Sidney's answer to all those who said he was sexless and square. This go-around Sidney's a suave, cigar-smoking rogue with a hip bachelor pad who falls for the maid and her good values. It was formula but it was sweet. It was also the last new Sidney flick for a while that would excite me.

I was eleven in 1968 and began rolling to the movies with friends from the neighborhood as I had with my mother. With his heroic turn in the ultra-macho *The Dirty Dozen* and lead roles in *Riot* and other ballsy efforts, Jim Brown was our new Saturday star. Sidney's films of the period (*Brother John*, *The Organization*) seemed too removed, way too precious a response to the street energy everybody, even we kids, were feeling.

In the late sixties and early seventies, Sidney's early films started popping up on local TV, giving me a new, more complicated view of the actor. Back in 1955 *The Blackboard Jungle* was viewed as a quite controversial study of juvenile delinquency in postwar America. It seemed corny to me as a seventies adolescent, but in its time Richard Brooks's trenchant film scared the hell out of America. The Sidney I saw in *The Blackboard Jungle* was a lithe, restless, smart but unmotivated kid with contempt for authority. This was someone I knew from the projects, someone I could project myself to be in a rebellious moment, precisely the kind of kid my mother had taken me to *To Sir with Love*, etc., to prevent me from becoming. Of course by the end Sidney's innate decency drove him to support Glenn Ford's courageous teacher versus Vic Morrow's protopunk. I knew Sidney in *The Blackboard Jungle* but I didn't recognize him.

The gap between the Sidney of *Guess* and *The Blackboard Jungle* was filled for me one night, maybe it was black history month, when channel nine had a special no-commercial-interruption airing of *A Raisin in the Sun*. We'd read Lorraine Hansberry's play in English class. Her picture was always part of any black literature poster along with Richard Wright, James Baldwin, Ralph Ellison, and Gwendolyn Brooks. Hansberry was just one of those "positive" people you were supposed to know and *Raisin* was what you were supposed to read (unlike the Donald Goines novels and *Players* magazines I was now regularly sampling).

But unlike white works on the "race question" like *Guess*, *Raisin* had a vibrancy and versimilitude that gave it life. I'd seen the family matriarch, Mother Younger, walking the streets of Brooklyn. The role of the frustrated wife, played here by Ruby Dee, I knew from real life too. Diana Sands's Beneatha, however, was a new character. Bright, articulate in the King's English, Afrocentric in a way that confounded her bourgie peers, and cute the way a woman caught up in finding herself always is, Beneatha was a black woman that the cinema still hasn't seen enough of. I didn't know it yet but I'd be chasing and, on occasion, catching women like Beneatha most of my life.

Sidney's Walter Lee, the troubled young husband and imperfect dad, whose poor judgment almost cost the Youngers their dreams, is someone I knew too well. My father had some of his zest and many of his faults. Like Walter Lee, the elder George fell in with bad companions. Like Walter Lee, he chafed under the restrictions of his job (Walter Lee was a chauffeur; my father a mailman). But for all their similarities Walter Lee and my father were separated by a crucial difference: my father split, Walter Lee came home and redeemed himself. In Walter Lee, Hansberry created one of the most complicated, multifaceted, yet ultimately optimistic male characters in American literature.

And Sidney eats him up. Playing a young and foolish man, the then thirty-four-year-old actor was riveting. His Walter Lee paces his family's south side shotgun apartment like a caged panther. Everything about him suggests a man in turmoil, a man with grandiose dreams but small means. Walter Lee is one of countless brothers who had reached maturity with the American dream dancing before them only to feel stunted by their lack of capital, which is certainly the adult male American nightmare. I loved this Sidney Poitier. He was so strong and vulnerable and ambitious, though he wasn't a guy you aspired to be. I figured Walter Lee was a stage you had to go through in order to end up Virgil Tibbs.

Buck and the Preacher was one of the last movies I remember seeing with my mother. By 1972 the Pitkin Theater was well beyond acceptable, reeking of mildew and urine. So we ventured up to a movie house in Crown Heights at Nostrand Avenue and then tree-lined Eastern Parkway (the theater is now the Philadelphia Church of God in Christ) where we'd seen Elvis Presley's *Kissin' Cousins* years ago. At this time Crown Heights was undergoing what

Brownsville had before—a mass exodus of its white ethnic popula-tion—but the local theater hadn't yet fallen victim to the shoddy management that inevitably accompanied it. I wish I could say this black Western (which Sidney directed) made a deeper impression on me than that earlier Elvis musical had, but with all honesty I can't. Rife with forgotten black history—black cowboys, runaway slaves resettling in the West, Native Americans aiding blacks—it struck me as convoluted and even a little dull. I'd seen Sam Peckinpah's *The Wild Bunch* a few years before and I judged every Western afterward by it. By that measure *Buck* was just so-so.

Moreover the consensus among my peers was that *Buck* wasn't as fly as *Shaft* or *Superfly* or *The Mack* and the slew of urban action flicks (*The French Connection*, etc.) we were gobbling up. I feel bad about not liking *Buck* now, but kids make entertainment judgments based on being entertained, not the cultural agenda of adults.

Apparently this new cinematic reality was not lost on Sidney. His authority as an icon had been eroded by blaxploitation's baaad bold brothers. At the same time a desire for more family-oriented films (e.g., *Sounder*, *Claudine*) was being expressed by those out-raged by blaxploitation's excesses. Even we young male hard-core action fans were tiring of chintzy blaxploitation production values and were voting with our wallets by abstaining from *Shaft's Big Score*, *Shaft in Africa*, and *Scream*, *Blacula*, *Scream*. In 1974 I was seventeen and movies were excuses for dates. Don't remember who I went with but I believe I saw *Uptown Saturday Night* at the Criterion Theater in Times Square (which to this day is a key venue for black movies). Sidney, as I noted, was no longer an icon. The irony, of course, is that now he had more control of his work than ever before. The film was developed by his production company, he picked the screenwriter (black theater alum) Richard Wesley, and directed it. No longer seeking to be the inspiring role model of *Heat*, Sidney on screen became an on-screen bumbler, an everyman who's new persona belied his behind-the-scenes power. In addition, the film itself worked as a satire of the blaxploitation genre that had made his retrenchment necessary. The film's gimmicky plot thrust working-class Sidney and his buddy Bill Cosby into a world of gangsters, con men, and cool people played by a great cast of Harry Belafonte, Calvin Lockhart, Roscoe Lee Browne, Richard Pryor, and

Paula Kelly. Though far from an inspired director, Sidney had already learned one lesson that served him well—when doing comedy keep the camera on the funny guy. In *Uptown*, as well as *Let's Do It Again* and *A Piece of the Action*, Sidney places his faith in Bill Cosby and provides the cigar-smoking comedian his best cinematic showcases. (The 1990 reunion was the remarkably unfunny *Ghost Dad*.) Later Sidney employed the same strategy in *Stir Crazy* with Richard Pryor and Gene Wilder, a buddy comedy that became the only $100 million-grossing film directed by an African-American.

By the time I'd reached adulthood the man who'd so influenced my childhood had basically disappeared from movie screens. He'd found refuge from the pressures of being "the" black actor as a director of comedies with little or no social relevance. In an age when Sean Connery, Clint Eastwood, and, to a lesser degree, Marlon Brando still worked with regularity, Sidney stepped back from center stage and no other black actor has quite filled his noble space. Maybe what he did is anachronistic or even impossible today. Still, I miss the dramatic Sidney and wish he'd work more often.

In the summer of 1991 I had a chance to finally meet Sidney Poitier. Out in Los Angeles working on a script, I got invited by the producer Sean Daniel to accompany him to a Nelson Mandela tribute at USC. It was my first big Hollywood event and, I would later learn, one of the rare integrated gatherings. As I walked into the main dining room, Sidney appeared before me. I was awestruck. Number one, the brother is a big man. He's well over six feet with a large head and a barrel chest. It wasn't just size that made him large, it was how he carried himself. That regal quality that leaped off the screen at me when I was a kid was no act. The man moved like a king. Everything and everyone around him seemed to shrink in relation to him, including yours truly. There was a moment when we were right next to each other.

Two filmmakers at a Hollywood fundraiser. Peers, you might say. I could have introduced myself and kicked it to him about the agony of development hell. You know, something real inside and knowing.

Instead I froze and just looked up at him, flashing back on Mr. Tibbs and Walter Lee Younger and the Saturdays his presence accompanied us to Chinese restaurants after viewing his flicks. I wished my mother were there, because if she had been I'd have lost no time introducing her to him. Then the moment was gone. He moved to his table where Harry Belafonte and Quincy Jones and that whole crew of long-standing Hollywood blacks held court with the great Mandela. I moved to my table in the back near midlevel development executives and fading R & B stars. I suppose I should have said something. Maybe I will one day. But Sidney Poitier and Nelson Mandela were too much for one summer night.

THE WHITE PLAGUE

At first taking out the garbage was an adventure. It was doing something for my mother. It was having a responsibility. It was a way to get out of our project apartment after dark and sneak down to visit my friend Junior down the hall. Then all of a sudden taking out the garbage wasn't fun anymore.

One night I went out our door and down the long corridor of our wing of the sixth floor. I made a left toward the elevators and standing right by them, with a brown bag held up to their noses, were two teenage males. One had his face damn near stuffed inside the bag. The other had his head cocked sideways trying to suck in whatever vapors escaped from around the edges of his partner's face. I stood there transfixed. The smell of rotting garbage, the noise of the elevator going up and down, and the chill of that autumn evening all stopped registering. These cats were sniffing glue, which I'd already been schooled to know was the vilest of vices. This was back in the age of model airplanes and I'd already been warned not to indulge innumerable times by my mother. "It'll rot your brain," she'd lectured. The mere sight of a clear bottle of Elmer's glue made me feel endangered.

So to see this duo enthusiastically engaged in destroying their precious brain cells was a serious shock to my prepubescent system. They looked up briefly from their activities. I made eye contact with them, but they sought none with me. Quickly their noses were again buried deep in that bag.

That was my first contact with the drug culture. In retrospect sniffing glue seems a juvenile vice, something that might be mentioned in *Mad* magazine or something that belongs to the age of horses and buggies or, at the very least, big-finned Caddies. But back then people thought the misuse of glue was a threat to our nation's youth, particularly to those of us living in what commentators then termed "slums." "Quaint" is a strange adjective to use to describe drug abuse but, looking back, that's the best way to characterize my first contact with it.

Within five years a true market explosion had occurred, and drugs of every kind—marijuana, heroin, cocaine, speedballs—had flowed into my neighborhood and turned the simple journey from my family's apartment to the incinerator into a nightly nerve-racking experience.

As sniffing glue gave way to reefer and reefer to the powerhouse addiction of heroin (roughly 1967 to 1972), the Tilden Projects grew ever more dangerous. Junkies would break the elevators or, almost as bad, knock out the lights in them. An inoperable elevator meant you took one of the two staircases to your apartment in our sixteen-story building. Junkies would lurk in staircases or in hallways like ours, shooting up or lying in wait to rip people off (after they'd knocked out the lights there, too). A day didn't go by in the early seventies when some tale of drug-related violence—a purse snatching, a car burglary, a shooting, a bloody murder—wasn't passed among the residents of the building. I had my first introduction to a feeling that would be a new urban constant—paranoia.

Every night from the time drugs hit Brownsville to the day my family moved to the short-lived safety of an integrated housing complex, taking out the garbage was a tension-inducing chore. Some nights, when the garbage load was light, I'd dash down to the incinerators and back, racing against my fear. But on others I'd have two or three bags to dump and be too loaded down to run. And, in the ancient days before plastic bags, paper shopping bags often broke. I'd stuff my garbage down (and often someone else's), all the time crazy paranoid about a junkie jumping out of a stairwell to shoot, stab, or do whatever.

In this environment the police went from role models (I remember envying the authority of traffic cops) to conspirators in the deterioration of our lives. Out of my sixth-floor window I had a beautiful view of Brownsville, especially the urban renewal that demolished scores of tenements. I used to see three and four police cars clustered together on a now empty side street, talking and sending out squad cars for Chinese food while junkies were snatching purses by the subway exit three blocks away.

Even more damning were the payoffs any child could witness. The elevated IRT line ran down Livonia Avenue past the projects. In the rusty metal beams that held the trains up were innumerable crooks and crevices. And inside them, brown paper bags, smaller but the same as the ones we used for garbage, were stuffed. One summer Saturday I sat for several hours after a modestly dressed black man placed a bag inside a beam below my window, then strolled away. My kid's instinct said, "Go grab it!" My ghetto knowledge said, "Don't get involved!" Then a patrol car rolled up, an officer got out, inspected the beam, grabbed the bag, and drove off. Maybe he'd received a tip about a mysterious bag? Maybe they'd intercepted a drug drop-off? Maybe I should have given the police the benefit of the doubt? Maybe I shouldn't have made the link between the junkies and the elevators and the brown bags, but I did. You see, I was wise to them all, because I'd been going to the movies.

During this period, a time when New York's public image plummeted from Mayor Lindsay's "Fun City" to the crime-ridden metropolis of Johnny Carson's nightly monologues, a series of films painted a bleak portrait of my city, one that fleshed out my childhood experiences and gave them a wider, sinister context. Some of the films are blaxploitation; some are considered classics. Together they created a tapestry of star-studded despair that mirrored the decay consuming much of my known world. For me *Superfly* and *Gordon's War*, along with the more celebrated *The Godfather*, *Serpico*, and *The French Connection*, flow into an epic narrative I titled *How the Mafia, the Cops, and Black Dealers Messed Up My Neighborhood*.

After all, what is *The Godfather* about? Yeah, it's an American epic about assimilation, loyalty, family, and the American dream, etc. Those are, as critics say, "the larger themes." However, the nuts and bolts of the plot is based on the real-world debate about whether or not the Mafia should mass-market heroin—with black folks at the center of the deal. As the head of one of the five families says at a crucial powwow, "They're animals anyway. Let them lose their souls."

That's why the noble Don Corleone is blasted outside his Genco Olive Oil company in Little Italy, that's why Fredo cries in the middle of the street, that's why Sonny gets his cap peeled at a Long Island toll station, and why, finally, Michael Corleone has to orchestrate the vengeful baptism of blood that climaxes *The Godfather*. You'll remember that Don Barzini wants to sell heroin in New York but Marlon Brando's noble Godfather is reluctant because he feels

his political and police connections will find it dangerous and dis-
tasteful. His qualms about dealing heroin are based on an actual
conflict in Mafia circles, though the debate wasn't nearly as high-
toned as Francis Ford Coppola, Al Pacino, and Marlon Brando
made it seem.

So the whole nexus of this great film turns on controlling the
dollars and destroying the souls of African-Americans. By the end
of *The Godfather*, as Pacino's Michael Corleone accepts greetings
from his assassins in his father's old office, Corleone-sanctioned
dope is now filling the streets of Harlem (with mall America soon to
follow). Fast-forward to *Serpico* and *The French Connection*, both
based on the real-life stories of crazed, heroic New York City cops.
These films posit a world where the white police establishment has
been so corrupted by dope dollars (*Serpico*), so outsmarted by drug
couriers (*The French Connection*), and is so morally weak (both
films) that they are helpless to prevent (though they eventually
profit from) heroin's conquest of New York.

The halls and alleys through which Pacino's Frank Serpico and
Gene Hackman's "Popeye" Doyle chase, woo, and fire guns are pri-
marily black and Puerto Rican. In an early character-establishing
scene Doyle, undercover in a Santa Claus suit, scares a dealer out of
a Harlem bar and then befuddles this black man with bullshit, con-
firming his street smarts and ability to "deal" with the blacks he's
supposed to be protecting. The cops that Serpico rats on before the
Knapp Commission for being "on the pad" are just like the cops
who picked up the brown bag from the subway beam. Literally and
metaphorically, the people and the streets that are the backdrops
for these two white heroes are dark and, both films suggest,
doomed from reel one.

In *The Godfather*, which is set mainly in the fifties, there are a
few corrupt white cops and many honorable crooks. In *The French
Connection* there are still a few good white men, yet in their zeal to
collar crooks they often blur the line between police work and
morality. In *Serpico* the corrupt cop, overwhelmingly white and ethnic, is now the norm; in fact now they are the crooks without
honor. That the protagonists of all these films were either Italian or
Irish were, from my kid's viewpoint, so perfect. These two groups
had been the subjects of scores of films about the city—its heroes,

its villains, its lifeblood—from the Hollywood B movies of the thirties right up to the seventies. And, in real life, the city had been theirs until the combination of black influx and drug importation began chasing them away.

That was crucial to the magic of blaxploitation. Coming as it did after the riots of the sixties and during the massive white flight of the Nixon years, blaxploitation presented an urban landscape where blacks were at the center of the universe and whites, while still impacting on our lives from outside the core community, were less important to our day-to-day lives except, of course, for the police. A movie like Gordon Parks Jr.'s *Superfly* was so mesmerizing precisely because it depicted the centrality of African-Americans, not just to the action genre, but to the sad saga of drugs. With his Cadillac El Dorado, big-brimmed hats, and lethal sideburns, Ron O'Neal's Priest was a glamorous vision of the commonplace drug wholesaler. No one I saw or knew in Brownsville was as fly as Priest. Part of Priest's cachet was that he sold cocaine, which was a more specialized market than heroin; part of it was that it was a movie.

More typical and more poignant is a tragicomic character in *Superfly* named Freddie. A roly-poly sad sack with a greedy girlfriend, Freddie was a black everyman who toiled rather ineffectively for Priest. When Freddie comes up short on some deals, Priest sends him to rip off a Mafia functionary in New Jersey. Later in the film he's beaten to death, which inspired the Curtis Mayfield classic "Freddie's Dead."

One of the chief appeals of blaxploitation's best films (and black film's current wave) was that by changing the point of view of a generic film you could capture, even fleetingly, some glimpse of our urban reality. Though Priest was the narrative's throughline, Freddie's role was crucial because he was a man locked by circumstance and greed into a lifestyle totally wrong for him. Freddie should have been home with his kids after his nine to five. Instead he was living out a destructive ghetto fantasy of empowerment. Tabloid hype notwithstanding, most drug dealers are not flamboyant or wealthy or resolutely menacing. For most selling drugs is a part-time job with no health insurance, no social security, and no long-term prospects. Freddie is killed by corrupt cops, cops controlled by Corleone types, cops unlike Popeye Doyle, cops testified against by Frank Serpico. Again, for me as a black audience member, the existence of nefarious policing was no hyperbole but a rendering of how blacks are squeezed by the police and how effectively they work as pawns of ruling ethnic elites.

The film that best blended all these themes of white corruption and black complicity in urban crime is an obscure flick titled *Across 110th Street*. A desperate trio of black men rob a Mafia-run numbers bank in Harlem (hence the title). At the same time a new black detective enters a traditionally white, traditionally corrupt precinct. Unlike *The French Connection* or *Superfly*, which respectively put a selfless white and a suave ghetto hustler at the center of a melodrama, *Across 110th Street* paints everyone who walks upon the screen—white and black—with the same tortured brush. While Yaphet Kotto's upwardly mobile cop would have been the hero of a typical blaxploitation effort or Anthony Quinn's fallen detective the focus of a regular ethnic New York police procedural, it is Antonio Fargas, as a vain and unstable robbery team member, who provides the most empathetic performance.

Fargas, who'd go on to some modest notoriety as the snitch Huggy Bear on *Starsky and Hutch*, was the quintessential black character actor. His jivey acting style, unjustified bravado, and wiry frame set off sparks in everything from *Putney Swope* to *Shaft*. (Years later he would parody himself in Keenen Ivory Wayans's blaxploitation spoof *I'm Gonna Git You Sucka*.) In *Across* he doesn't lie low with the cash as cautioned, but spends it on hookers and coke at a Harlem brothel. His fate is to squeal on his friends before being castrated by Mafia enforcer Tony Franciosa. In the struggle between white corruption and black criminality that underpins so many of the films I watched during this period, Fargas joins Freddie as a forgotten victim in the battle.

There are other films that fit into this druggy narrative: *Crazy Joe*, a biography of a Mafia figure, Joey Gallo, whose liaison with black criminals (represented by Fred Williamson) got him assassinated by the old Don Corleone–era Dons; *The Mack*, which pits Max Julien's black Oakland pimp in a struggle with two of the most depraved white cops in the entire blaxploitation genre; *Shaft*, the story of a black private dick who aids a black gangster in freeing his kidnapped daughter from the Mafia.

One of the least remembered but most intriguing of these films was the urban fantasy *Gordon's War*. In it a group of Vietnam veterans come home to a Harlem deluged with dope. In response they start a vigilante squad against dealers. Bringing credibility to this fanciful premise is Paul Winfield as the righteous Gordon.

The film's deep problem, of course, is that so many of the Vietnam vets came back, not as crusaders, but as addicts or traffickers. Easy access (you could buy heroin right outside many army bases in 'Nam) and the intense war situation brought home so many profoundly damaged. A great many soldiers never recovered from that conflict and heroin was a prime reason. Contacts made in Asia by black GIs contributed to the Golden Triangle trade that transmitted the white plague from Thailand and 'Nam into veins in Detroit, Newark, Chicago, and Brownsville.

I remember how many of the junkies begging for quarters at the subway and snatching purses on project staircases were wearing green army jackets with names of places in 'Nam written on them. Men who were supposed to be fathers and leaders in our communities came back and, in too many cases, helped accelerate the chaos. If you combine the number of black men killed in 'Nam with the number who came back addicted, you'd have a damn good clue as to why black families have been on the ropes since the sixties. There's a big hole in the chain of African-American life that the nexus of that war and drug addiction contributed to. *Gordon's War* didn't explain that, but then no one really has.

Sometime during high school I discovered that there was more to Manhattan than Times Square. For a child steeped in moviegoing on Forty-second Street this was a major move forward. A friend introduced me to *The Village Voice* and through the *Voice* I learned about clubs and cafes in Greenwich Village. A high school buddy shanghaied me to the classy East Side, where I first encountered Bloomingdale's and a raft of retailers that bore no resemblance to Pitkin Avenue. Aside from Bloomingdale's I found that the Baronet and Coronet, along with their next-door neighbors, the Cinema I and II, featured the "quality" fare and foreign films that avoided Times Square. Later I began visiting revival houses in the Village—the Bleecker Street Cinema, Theatre 80, and the Elgin on Eighth Avenue with its midnight movies. The Playboy Theater on Fifty-seventh Street on the West Side even had a $1 movie policy on Saturday afternoons, perfect for my high school budget.

It became a ritual that every Friday I'd survey the *Voice* listings, seeking out childhood favorites (*The Godfather* films), detective films (*The Big Sleep*, *The Maltese Falcon*), or rare black-themed double features (*Stormy Weather*, *Cabin in the Sky*). Along with the listings, I started reading the *Voice* reviews and was particularly taken with Andrew Sarris's film reviews and Robert Christgau's complicated rock criticism in the "Riffs" section. I didn't know then that Sarris had helped refine the "auteur theory" of films that was so often alluded to in the paper's reviews, nor that Christgau was a pioneer in taking pop music seriously. During my years at Tilden High School and into my freshman year at St. John's University, I read as much criticism as I could consume. I was in college when I purchased Greil Marcus's *Mystery Train*, a supremely ambitious and largely satisfying look at six great rock 'n' roll artists in the context of American history. While his fixation with Elvis Presley left me cold, Marcus's chapter on Sly Stone was a revelation. Marcus discussed the great bandleader in connection with the black liberation struggle, the white rock audience's relationship to black icons, and America's fear/fixation with "bad niggers." Marcus's point of departure was the legend of Staggerlee, a twisted, violent mythological character whose tale has been passed in story and song throughout this century. The Sly chapter also featured a detailed delving into Sly's dark, druggy masterpiece "There's a Riot Goin' On."

In a surprising sidebar Marcus found time for a detailed description of the aesthetic conflict waged between the makers of blaxploitation films and the more humanistic black music of the early seventies. That the soundtracks for these films were often at odds with the films they supported (e.g., *Superfly*) was not lost on Marcus.

The process really stretched me intellectually. The idea that the cultural products of my young life—from the *Superfly* soundtrack to the O'Jays' *Ship Ahoy* album to the Panther paper—were not disconnected but part of an on-going dialogue that reflected and/or molded their time seemed right to me.

I eventually submitted a few music essays to Christgau at the *Voice*. I got a short letter back on the first one. I got a postcard with a typewritten response on the second one. On the third one I got a form letter on a small postcard. Detecting a pattern of diminishing returns, I turned elsewhere and wrangled an interview at the *Amsterdam News*. I was a sophomore at St. John's then and, through a college program, was able to hook up three college credits for getting an internship at the *Am News*. So at nineteen I was working after school at the Harlem weekly.

The *Am News*, like most black newspapers, was understaffed in many areas. I was interested in writing about music but between staffers, freelancers, and gossip columnists that scene was covered. The city's fertile black theater community was generating lots of activity and getting much well-deserved ink. The networks deluged the paper with press releases, photos, and other promotional crap if a black actor or actress so much as burped in a scene. Theatrical film was actually the low slot on the paper's art totem pole. Blaxploitation had bitten the dust, and with it went any urgency about film coverage. But the *Am News* still got ads for action flicks (e.g., the black *Rocky* ad that showed Carl Weathers's Apollo Creed trading blows with Sylvester Stallone) and regularly ran studio press releases. James P. Murray, who'd held down the critic's spot during the blaxploitation era, had split for a gig in NBC's publicity department after becoming the first black member of the New York Film Critics Circle and writing a book on the seventies black film boom. Since his exit the job had been passed around. So I wasn't surprised that one afternoon an editor told me to review a screening of *Pipe Dreams*, a film about blacks working on the Alaskan pipeline starring the singer Gladys Knight. Feeling this might work as a side door into music writing, I hurried on downtown.

Pipe Dreams was amateurish, although Gladys Knight acquitted herself well and I got my first review out of it. The highlight of the experience, however, was meeting D. Parke Gibson, a heavyset man in his forties who'd written a book on the untapped potential of the black consumer market. He'd been hired to help the film's producers tap into just that market. Though his efforts were wasted on *Pipe Dreams*, the chance to talk with Gibson (and reading his book) made the movie worth my while. Next I was sent to review *Brothers*, a Warner Bros. fictionalization of the romance between Angela Davis and George Jackson. As you can imagine, the politics (not the sex) were bowdlerized. Vonetta McGee made for a sexy Davis and Ron O'Neal, in one of his first post-*Superfly* roles, was quite touching as a convict who politicizes Bernie Casey's Jackson.

Thus, by default, for much of the next two years I was the chief film critic at the city's leading black weekly. I furiously read every book of criticism I could find, signed up for every film course St. John's offered, and tried to act as mature as possible whenever I attended screenings. At one point I even started smoking a pipe, a tactic, I'm sure you're not shocked to hear, that only made me the target of laughter in the *Am News* offices. The black film histories by Donald Bogle (*Toms, Coons, Mulattoes, Mammies & Bucks*) and Thomas Cripps (*Slow Fade to Black*) were my bibles. Archivist Pearl Bowser was showing much of Oscar Micheaux's still existing work around the city, opening my eyes to the world of alternative black filmmaking that existed as early as the twenties outside Hollywood. I don't think I realized how lucky I was except when I thought how much money I was saving on dates. The few African-Americans I encountered in the film biz were publicists such as the late James Johnson at Paramount and Vicki Horsford at Columbia (sister of actress Anna Maria), both of whom kindly looked out for me. Johnson even got me on my first junket—a trip to Las Vegas's MGM Grand for the football flick *North Dallas Forty*. Twenty years old in Vegas with a gaudy burgundy and leopard trim hotel suite was, as we said at the time, da joint.

I made it to two historic premieres, *Close Encounters of the Third Kind* and *Apocalypse Now*, both held in the seventy-millimeter Dolby splendor of the magnificent Zeigfeld Theater. At the *Apocalypse Now* junket at the Plaza Hotel I met a then-teenaged Larry Fishburne, who spent much of our interview time together bouncing around the room like a rubber ball. When he calmed down I remember we talked as much about *Cornbread, Earl and Me* as Coppola's epic. Screenwriter-turned-director Paul Schrader became a personal favorite, especially with *Blue Collar* and *American Gigolo*, the latter being the film that taught me what little I know about style.

One of my great discoveries during this time was Akira Kurosawa. A film class professor at St. John's screened *Yojimbo* and I immediately realized I was seeing an example of how powerfully the culture of a nonwhite world could be translated cinematically. Before clicking on the projector the professor primed us with the vital info that Hollywood had been ripping off Kurosawa for years: *The Magnificent Seven* came from *The Seven Samurai*, *Yojimbo* had been adapted into *A Stranger in Town* and the imagery of George Lucas's *Star Wars* was deeply influenced by Kurosawa's painterly compositions.

Kurosawa's great star Toshiro Mifune was, we were told, the Japanese Clint Eastwood. I was hooked by *Yojimbo*'s opening scene where Mifune's cynical mentorless samurai encounters a mangy dog with a man's severed hand clutched in its mouth. It's a sinister, threatening, comical image that establishes Kurosawa's command and viewpoint. Compared to Eastwood's laconic, stoic gunslinger Mifune's face is infinitely more animated. His cocky walk and jangling physique reminded me of a past-prime basketball star still not willing to be pushed off court. Kurosawa's dark humor and Mifune's funky presence drew me in.

The experience was deepened by Kurosawa's amazing framing—I'd never seen anyone use the movie screen with such compositional rigor—and the rich culture I was introduced to. I was impressed by the fact that Japan had an aesthetically well-developed, nonwhite world. They had their own drinks, food, clothes, standards of beauty, music, religion, and history, all of which were manifest in *Yojimbo*. For all the Western techniques Kurosawa exploited, there was a pride in things Japanese that underpinned the film.

Unlike the Hollywood and European films I'd been weaned on, the nonwhite actors were not "the other," the foreigner, the brunt of the joke or the "symbol" of pathology, acceptance, or rebellion in a world where white skin dominated. My beloved kung fu flicks had shown Asian characters as potent and assertive, but Kurosawa's craft and seriousness, of course, made those Forty-second Street features seem like jokes. That Kurosawa and company weren't black didn't matter to me. That they weren't white did. He had told his own story using tools that whites had, apparently, reserved for themselves. If a Japanese man could do that, then a black person could too.

I had closely monitored the career of black director Michael Schultz (*Cooley High* and *Car Wash*), who, I naively thought, could be our Kurosawa. I loved his Richard Pryor vehicle *Which Way Is Up?* but *Greased Lightning* was at best so-so. However, the disaster that was *Sgt. Pepper's Lonely Hearts Club Band* not only ruined the recording careers of Peter Frampton and the Bee Gees, but really sent Schultz's directing career into a tailspin. The momentum Schultz had built from his early films was never fully recovered.

What I didn't yet understand is that you can't be a real rebel in the black nationalists' sense, or be completely oppositional within the Hollywood system of compromise. Given a chance to see a wide range of movies, I couldn't believe how uninspired, unoriginal, and ungainly most Hollywood flicks were or how scattered were the black roles in them. Where were all those actors I'd grown up watching just five years before? For African-Americans, Hollywood films of the late seventies were a cinematic wasteland with *Rocky* series regular Carl Weathers one of the few sure of a gig from year to year. And black women had it worse. Cicely Tyson became a made-for-TV movie queen but the Rosalind Cashes, Pam Griers, Vonetta McGees were largely invisible. Only the comic-turned-actor Richard Pryor stood shakily between black folks and a whitewashed Saturday night at the movies.

RICHARD & ME

I was carrying my notepad, my tape recorder, and wearing my best beige summer jacket. Riding the subway into the city I studied my questions again and again. I was as nervous as a filly at the Preakness, and I had a right to be. I was going to interview Richard Pryor for the *Amsterdam News*. What could top that? What if the movie he was promoting, *Greased Lightning*, a biopic of black stock-car pioneer Wendell Scott, was as mild as skim milk? I knew he was the funniest motherfucker on the planet, had all his albums, and couldn't wait to laugh real hard during our time together.

But instead of the private interview I'd anticipated, I walked into a dining room with three tables full of journalists, all staring expectantly at the door. Check that: three tables of *black* journalists. Where the white press got private time with Pryor, the black press had been convened for a group grope, typical of how white publicity firms traditionally treat (or mistreat) African-American media, even when they're dealing with an African-American subject.

I settled in next to a friend from another black weekly, the *Black American*. He was as hyped as I about the interview prospect; he had as many questions as I did. Pryor appeared with a publicist and a bodyguard at the doorway. He looked like he'd just gotten out of bed and that his dreams had not been pleasant. The comedian was guided to our table. A plate of food was slid before him. Pryor proceeded to eat.

Being enthusiastic and young I peppered Pryor with questions. My friend from the *Black American*, not as young but equally enthusiastic, queried Pryor too. In lieu of answers Pryor stared, grunted, and generally generated a wave of nonverbal hostility. When his meal was finished and our fifteen minutes had elapsed, Pryor was escorted to table number two where two comely female writers awaited. Within two minutes the comatose comic had revived and the sound of women's laughter floated over toward the frustrated cinephiles back at table number one.

The publicist whispered that after Pryor finished at table number three we'd all get another crack at him. I was willing to wait. By table number three Pryor was wide awake and was jesting happily with a nitwit newsman from the local black FM station. By now I was fuming. My professional ego, quite fragile in my days as a rookie scribe, had been badly bruised. Moreover, I already had developed a profound intolerance of star eccentricities. The more Pryor cooperated with the other tables, including people I thought of as incompetent, like the radio guy, the more pissed I became. So I left.

I didn't think Pryor noticed, though later the *Black American* writer told me he asked, "Where was the *Amsterdam News* guy?" By that time I had pouted my way over to the subway. It was, for me, a missed opportunity. I wasn't self-aware enough to realize how much I wanted Pryor to acknowledge me. Shows how unprepared I really was. Why in the world would I expect the man who'd made *That Nigger's Crazy* or *Craps—After Hours* to conform to interview niceties? That was never what this brother was about.

Nobody mentions this anymore, but Richard Pryor was once as notorious in the black community as Snoop Doggy Dogg or Luther Campbell. That he had the temerity to use the "N" word in an album title back in 1974 was considered quite "negative" in the days when the idea of a monolithic "positive" black image was unchallenged. On the heels of sixties crossover icons like Sidney Poitier, Bill Cosby, and Motown, Pryor had another take on mass success. As rap did a generation later, Pryor reached whites with an in-your-face use of "nigger." His ghetto characters, scatological references and florid profanity, hos, pimps, and junkies were early staples of his humor. Raw was his calling card.

Again, like subsequent hip-hoppers, Pryor developed both a loyal black constituency and a young hip white audience. Where Cosby and Sidney and Motown penetrated the American suburban mainstream, Pryor's rebellious spirit and drug fixations put him in sync with its white, often urban, counterculture. White Pryor fans had a lot of the same attitudes as those who'd helped Jimi Hendrix cross over as an icon, while his black fans were the young people for whom Redd Foxx, Moms Mabley, Wildman Steve, and the rest of the chitlin' circuit comics were either too old-fashioned or just plain too old.

Possession of *That Nigger's Crazy* back then was as crucial a signifier of hipness as Ice Cube's *AmeriKKKa's Most Wanted* would be in 1990. My friends and I would sit and listen to it, sipping beer or wine and smoking herb as if the album were as dense as *Stairway to Heaven* or Stevie Wonder's *Inner Visions*. Cheech and Chong's whole career was built on being smokable comedians. So to a great degree was George Carlin's. But the range of Pryor's genius defied being boxed in by druggies, black cultural nationalists, or cross-cultural hipsters of my persuasion.

That Pryor apparently lost his mind in Hollywood, like so many before him, is sad not simply in the way all human loss is sad; it was a tragedy of enormous proportions for African-Americans. I've always considered Pryor one of the greatest African-American writers. His characters were very detailed and always based on reality, yet surreal in a way you might find in books by Ralph Ellison, Zora Neale Hurston, or Chester Himes. His understanding of the pathology of the junkie and the allure of addiction (to cocaine, to alcohol, to sex) made him more than a funny man. As a performer Pryor not only did characters; he could also animate objects, breathing life into punctured tires, car engines, and seductive crack pipes.

My favorite character was Mudbone, a grizzled street veteran all too happy to dispense wisdom collected at the bad end of a bottle. In black lore winos are much more benign figures than junkies. Once fixtures in urban America, they were replaced menacingly in the seventies by heroin addicts as the community's street-corner tribe. In his famous "the wino and the junkie" routine, Pryor managed to capture that tragic transition in black culture where dope overwhelmed the community. Where the more folksy (and more romanticized) wino is still connected to his soul, the junkie's senses are so dulled that he can barely speak anymore, much less understand the wino's wisdom. There is no wisdom for the junkie—only a strange deathly limbo that will infect all around him or her.

"The wino and the junkie" is emblematic of the kind of multi-layered work that made Pryor's comedy so powerful. And it is precisely because of this oft-displayed brilliance that his film career was such a waste. Aside from the three concert films (*Richard Pryor Live in Concert*, *Richard Pryor Live on the Sunset Strip*, *Here and Now*), which capture the master in his element, his Hollywood work can by and large be praised only if you judge it in slivers. If you fast-forward your VCR through the crap that makes up *Critical

Condition, *The Toy*, and *Moving* you'll find a chuckle or two. Going back to his earlier work (the closer to his days as a pure stand-up, the less mannered were his performances) there are clips aplenty for a Pryor montage—Daddy Rich in *Car Wash*, Piano Man in *Lady Sings the Blues*, a manic con man in *Silver Streak*, and the pimp's comic sidekick in *The Mack*. For me the only two totally satisfying nonconcert films Pryor made are the drama *Blue Collar* and the comedy *Which Way Is Up?*

Blue Collar was co-written and co-directed by one of my favorite filmmakers, the rigorously intellectual and often perverse Paul Schrader. He'd already written *Taxi Driver* and would go on to direct *American Gigolo*, *Hardcore*, and other films that depict men caught between decadence and grace. In *Blue Collar* Pryor plays a Detroit auto assembly-line worker burdened with kids, debt, and limited prospects. Along with his production-line pals, Harvey Keitel and Yaphet Kotto, Pryor steals cash from the offices of the corrupt union local. The powers that be within the union, company, and government deal with each thief differently. Kotto is murdered. Keitel is forced to inform for the feds. Pryor is purchased by the status quo and winds up a corrupt cog in the machine of the very enterprise they ripped off.

In Schrader's screenplay Pryor's character is an economic, not social, rebel. All he ever really wanted was to get into the system, not to destroy it. When offered a chance to sell out, to become the token black floor supervisor and do better by his family, Pryor jumps at it. There is a complexity to this man's strengths and weaknesses that Pryor totally understands. The hostility that smolders under Pryor's stand-up humor is given free reign in a character trapped between responsibility and desire. He goes from being a bedeviled man sitting in a cluttered living room with kids roaming about to a cold, sarcastic member of the establishment that once oppressed him. The role reversal is frightening. The great thing about Pryor in *Blue Collar* is that he doesn't become a classic Uncle Tom. He's a more contemporary, subtler manifestation of that archetype. He's no docile accommodationist. The anger of the underclass still boils within—but it is the anger to get paid.

Pryor depicts him as grateful to the white man. He simply becomes disdainful of those, white and black, who haven't played the game as well as he. In the film's final scene, Keitel and Pryor face off in a shouting match that resonates with, but doesn't unrealistically resolve, the class conflicts that underlie *Blue Collar*. Years later Pryor would be rightly criticized for playing so many wimpy insecure characters. But for this shining moment Pryor is as cocksure as he'd ever be. As a warrior for capitalism he leaps at Keitel with a fury his acting never displayed on screen again.

Which Way Is Up?, based on Italian director Lina Wertmuller's *The Seduction of Mimi*, had as its protagonist another sellout. Leroy Jones is a man whose life as a migrant worker puts him in the way of things—picketing strikers, lusty women, and Mr. Man, a mysterious power broker. Pryor is again a capitalist tool, but here the plot is completely subservient to the humor. *Which Way Is Up?* was the third of four Pryor films directed by Michael Schultz (the others were *Car Wash*, *Greased Lightning*, and later *Bustin' Loose*) and was the best of the bunch.

In *Which* Pryor defined the jittery, beleaguered fellow that became his standard on-screen approach. In addition Pryor essayed two other roles: he played a morally corrupt preacher, Reverend Lenox Thomas (Pryor's middle names), familiar from his stand-up act; and the father of Pryor's character who's the closest Pryor came to an on-screen Mudbone. Assertive, profane, and screamingly funny as this decidedly foul-mouthed Papa, Prior made me sad to think he never dedicated an entire movie to this shrewd, crusty old man. *Which* is rife with silly sexual sight gags. One involves Margaret Avery, as Pryor's long-abandoned wife, who turns into a dominatrix to arouse her husband's desire, utilizing whips, chains, and a great big black dildo stuck in Pryor's butt to do the job. Marilyn Coleman plays a religious woman who's seduced by Pryor in her trailer home. The sight gag has the trailer bouncing up and down in time to their lovemaking (a gag used a few years later by director Carl Reiner and Steve Martin in *The Jerk*).

Which was hilarious and was enjoyed by most of the young black folks I knew. But it got mediocre-to-bad reviews from the mainstream press, and I know why. I first saw *Which* in a Universal screening room on Park Avenue with a collection of white New York reviewers. I was literally the only person laughing at many jokes. It was embarrassing to bust out with a loud guffaw only to hear it answered by a silence that announced I had bad taste. I split the screening room confused. I thought *Which* was damn funny. Yet all those movie pros sat stone-faced.

After *Which* opened I went down to Forty-second Street to a crappy little multiplex on the south side of the street. Squeezed into a narrow room with bad popcorn and a bunch of black and Puerto Rican kids, I roared even more than before—and this time I wasn't alone. The dildo scene rocked the house. Handslapping was rampant. People were still talking back to the screen about it two scenes later. Watching *Which* on the Deuce actually enriched its ribald humor. The film's faults were still apparent but those jokes flew.

After the movie, I stood at the Nedick's on Forty-second Street and Seventh Avenue (same one that's in *Shaft*) and pondered the difference between those two viewings. Pryor's stand-up humor, smart and deep, cut across all kinds of racial and social barriers. *Which* wasn't nearly as smart or insightful. It was, however, raw and visual and unapologetically working-class. It was the first time I'd really seen the gap between white critical opinion and black working-class taste so graphically illustrated. And it wouldn't be the last time.

Pryor was really the only African-American film star whose career was spawned during the blaxploitation era and who continued on as a leading man after that tide had ebbed. His now legendary drug habit notwithstanding, Hollywood never lost faith in his drawing power in the seventies while consistently misusing his talent. It is also important not to absolve Pryor of his guilt for agreeing to prepackaged crap like *Superman III*, for which he was paid $4 million in 1983, and which he had to know was unredeemable at any price. Pryor's immense talent (and the cajoling of his black attorney David Franklin) earned him the most unique deal any African-American has ever received in Hollywood. In 1983 Columbia Pictures head Guy McElwaine agreed to finance Pryor's Indigo Films to the tune of $40 million. That money was to be used to produce four movies including those that Pryor would write and direct. Pryor hired his main man, Jim Brown, as president and actress Shelia Frazier as head of development.

The good news was that young talent producers like George (*New Jack City*) Jackson and director-actor Robert (*Hollywood*

Shuffle) Townsend got some early industry experience through Indigo. The script that eventually became Clint Eastwood's *Bird*, originally intended for Pryor, passed through Indigo as well.

The bad news is that Indigo never really got off the ground. The only films to reach theaters bearing the Indigo Productions logo were his third concert film and his directorial effort *Jo Jo Dancer, Your Life Is Calling*, an uneven effort that at least had the ambition of Pryor's stand-up to recommend it.

Indigo was a classic case of the Peter principle. The comic's success had earned him the clout $40 million represents. Yet nothing about Pryor's life prepared him for the responsibility of running a production company. What drug addict is suited to be a boss? In December 1983 Brown was fired. Within two years Indigo was history—just in time for a black film renaissance to emerge from the underground.

THE BLACK FILMMAKER FOUNDATION

One day in 1978 several serious-looking brothers came by to meet with me at the *Am News*. Wearing Afros of various lengths and considerable facial hair, they sat sternly before me and spoke with the earnestness of true believers. They were the founders of a new nonprofit organization named the Black Filmmaker Foundation. Their goal was to put black independent film on the black cultural map.

As I noted earlier, at the *Am News* and in most black media at this point, films were not a big priority. By definition the non-Hollywood black film was way down the pecking order. These films generated no advertising. They had no stars. They couldn't be seen at local movie houses. The black intelligentsia focused most of its enthusiasm on the booming field of black women's literature and supporting live theater like the Negro Ensemble Company which had been presenting outstanding works—*Home*, *A Soldier's Play*, and *Last Breeze of Summer*.

Not in the African-American art mainstream and not accessible to the masses, black independent films stood at a strange angle to the community they tried to reflect. And, to be completely honest, many of the films were slow going. After the *Sweet Sweetback's Baadasssss Song* breakthrough, there was a definite backlash against the raw elements, moral ambiguity, and ghettocentricity of that work by black independents. Despite its success *Sweetback* was perceived by many cineasts as a politically retrograde work.

In part as a response to this, most of the black indie films I saw, whether documentaries or fictional works, were overwhelmingly righteous in their Marxist leanings, civil rights era nostalgia, or the glorification of black nationalist discourse. Any way you looked at it they were often extremely didactic. Films like Haile Gerima's *Harvest 3000 Years* (about a welfare mother's struggle to make a life for her daughter and herself) were strongly written and politically pointed but unexciting viewing for the politically unaware. But you can't ignore the fact that, even with problems of tedium or didacticism, these films were rife with details, observations, and attitudes about African-American life that Hollywood didn't care about. Even the most leisurely paced black indie film usually ended up projecting some heretofore unfilmed aspect of African-American life.

The most brilliant example, one that properly balanced the needs of politics and filmmaking, was Charles Burnett's *Killer of Sheep*, a feature-length look at a disaffected slaughterhouse worker in Watts. Shot on location in black and white, it had the grit and weight of the post–World War II Italian neorealistic movement. A slow dance between the worker and his sexually dissatisfied wife, choreographed to Dinah Washington's "This Bitter Earth," was as emotionally complex a moment as I'd seen on screen involving a black couple. Love, passion, impotence, and anxiety were all smartly captured by Burnett's use of music and framing. In his sensitive hands *Killer of Sheep* became one of the stellar achievements of African-American direction.

The BFF introduced me and the *Am News* readers to this world of filmmaking. Warrington Hudlin, a sharp Yale philosophy major and fine cinema vérité documentary maker, was the BFF executive director and chief cheerleader. Out of a small office on Fourteenth Street in Manhattan, the BFF developed a black indie film distribution network that made many of these works available to community groups around the country. In conjunction with New York City, the BFF worked as a cinematic jazzmobile by bringing showings of indie films to parks around New York.

In another phase of this outreach program, the BFF went to other nontraditional venues. One of my fondest memories is seeing Charles Lane's delightful silent short, *A Place in Time*, at the then hot Othello's disco on Eighth Avenue and Thirty-fifth Street. The contrast of Lane's sweet-natured film about a struggling street artist and the disco's let's-get-busy decor still makes me smile. I met a lot of dedicated people during this time. Some have gone on to make well-known features, some became teachers or technicians, and many are still pursuing their own non-Hollywood agenda. Knee-deep in the era of Pryor, they kept the dream of alternative black film alive in the years between Van Peebles and Lee.

My career as a film critic ended abruptly in 1980. I'd been out of college for less than a year when the *Am News* made a series of austerity cuts. My $91 every two weeks for writing film and sports was $91 too much.

Twenty-one and living in my first apartment, I was no longer in

Kansas. I was in Queens with very little income. Luckily I'd used my time at the *Am News* to make contacts in music journalism. I was freelancing and had this crazy dream of writing a book about Motown Records, a company whose journey from music to movies seemed like an apt metaphor for the African-American obsession with acceptance. For the next few years, however, books and films both took a backseat to stayin' alive.

Part Two

MAKING MOVIES
1970–1986

1970

Melvin Van Peebles, the first black auteur, directs *Watermelon Man* for Columbia Pictures, the farcical story of a white bigot who wakes up black one horrifying morning. Well played by Godfrey Cambridge. (Courtesy of Columbia Records.)

Ossie Davis directs the hit adaptation of Chester Himes's *Cotton Comes to Harlem* that stars Raymond St. Jacques and Godfrey Cambridge as Himes's black detectives Coffin Ed and Gravedigger Jones. Redd Foxx steals the show as a shrewd homeless man. Himes's Harlem detective novels, all first published to critical acclaim in France before reaching America, are unacknowledged inspirations for the blaxploitation's cartoony characters, though almost every one of the subsequent films lacked Himes's bitter wit.

Ossie Davis also helps found the production company Third World Cinema, using a $200,000 grant from the U.S. Manpower Career & Development Agency. Third World Cinema will go on to train many blacks and Hispanics for film and television production jobs.

Harry Belafonte stars in and his company produces *The Angel Levine*, a drama-fantasy in which the actor-singer plays Zero Mostel's guardian angel. Black playwright Bill Gunn co-wrote. Gunn, an actor turned writer, then makes the move into directing with *Stop*, a Warner Bros. feature that the studio shelves after viewing the rough cut.

The Landlord, based on a Kristin Hunter novel, centers around an interracial romance between Diana Sands and Beau Bridges. Pearl Bailey and
Lou Gossett also appear.

The Great White Hope, based on the hit Broadway play and starring
James Earl Jones, costs $6 million and brings in less than a million.
Variety observed that blacks "don't cotton to such pix, as . . . they feature
blacks in a losing light."

Bill Gunn's *Ganja & Hess*, a complex study of vampirism, sex, and spiri-
tualism, is fitfully distributed, recut, and often retitled (e.g., *Blood
Couple*). Duane Jones, who worked previously in *Night of the Living
Dead*, plays this film's elegant vampire. The film's mangling becomes a
cause célèbre for many black intellectuals. Critic James Monaco said, "If
Sweetback is *Native Son*, then *Ganja & Hess* is *Invisible Man*," and that
it was "the most complicated, intriguing, subtle, sophisticated, and passionate" black film of the seventies.

1971

One-fourth of all films in production are black-oriented after the unexpected success of Van Peebles's *Sweet Sweetback's Baadasssss Song*. The
film opens in scattered theaters around the country to critical amazement
and big black box office. Van Peebles even writes a book about the making of the film, the first "Making of" book by an African-American. By
focusing on a black stud's murder of two brutal white policemen, Van
Peebles dramatizes two previously taboo film subjects: justifiable black
suspicion of police authority in their communities and unbridled black
sexuality. Though essentially a European art film set in Watts, the film's
unrepentant tone struck a deep chord in everyone who saw it. Reportedly
Sweetback grossed $10 million. Just as *Easy Rider* had turned Hollywood
on to the youth audience a few years before, *Sweetback* announced to
the studios that there was money in the black audience.

In *The Omega Man,* black actress Rosalind Cash plays the female love
interest to Charlton Heston.

Gordon Parks Sr. directs Richard Roundtree in *Shaft*. Isaac Hayes composed an Oscar-winning score. Roundtree is paid $13,500. The film as

Isaac Hayes (left) and Gordon Parks Sr. scoring Shaft. (Courtesy of Stax Records.)

- the model for the black mainstream hero flick is established by Parks's atmospheric direction, Roundtree's trend-setting wardrobe, and Hayes's state-of-the-art soul meets jazz compositions. *Shaft* establishes several recurring blaxploitation themes: black nationalists are depicted as inept, if well meaning, supporting characters; young women, of all colors, are sexual pawns or playthings; white and black mobsters are in constant collaboration and conflict.

- Ossie Davis gives up 40 percent of Third World Cinema to a community group to qualify for a Model Cities grant of $400,000. During Nixon's second term, Model Cities and other Great Society programs would be terminated. Davis himself would eventually turn his full-time attention back to directing and acting, though Third World Cinema would go on to produce *Greased Lightning* and *Claudine*. This year Davis would direct *Kongi's Harvest*, a little-seen African drama scripted by future Nobel Prize winner Wole Soyinka.

- In *Emitai* Ousmane Sembène explores the evil impact of colonialism in Africa through the prism of a historical fact. During World War II the French army, desperate for reinforcements, kidnaps at gunpoint the young men of nonnationalized Senegalese tribes. To his credit Sembène doesn't paint the French as total villains, but finds cowardice and vanity on all sides of the situation. Sembène is more than a polemicist. His use of spatial relationships to communicate meaning is both shrewd and thrilling.

- Star and producer Sidney Poitier takes over direction of *Buck and the Preacher* two weeks into production. His longtime friends Harry

Belafonte and Ruby Dee provide support in this breakthrough look at blacks in the old West.

1972

Gordon Parks Sr. directs *Superfly*, which sets the tone for the black criminal as antihero that would affect not just other blaxploitation films, but rap music two decades later. Where *Shaft* was a typical detective flick in blackface, *Superfly*'s cocaine dealer was a more romantic, conflicted figure whose slang and clothes cut deeper than *Shaft* into the black community's psyche. Curtis Mayfield's score was, arguably, the single greatest black pop effort of the decade.

The glorification of Priest, played by Ron O'Neal, was profound and still stirs young people to this day. Gordon Parks Sr.'s photography is showcased in a sequence that illustrates cocaine's insidious flow through our society.

Trouble Man, starring Robert Hooks, has a brilliant title song written and sung by Marvin Gaye. Veteran actor Ivan Dixon directed this typical detective flick.

Black Gunn with Jim Brown is another *Shaft* variation. What distinguishes it is the use of a slew of other jocks, including pitcher Vida Blue and footballers Timmy Brown, Bernie Casey, Gene Washington, and Deacon Jones. Much as rappers are the black film acting gimmick of the nineties, black athletes served the same role in the seventies.

Lady Sings the Blues is Motown's flashy move into Holly-wood. Berry Gordy co-produced, Diana Ross starred as Billie Holiday, Billy Dee Williams was the black heartthrob, Richard Pryor was heartbreaking as "Piano Man," and Suzanne De Passe co-wrote the Oscar-nominated script. It wasn't really Holiday's life, but it was as slick as any Supremes' love song.

Sounder, the story of a black family during the Depression, is probably the best black drama of the period. Sensitively directed by Martin Ritt, it stars Oscar nominees Cicely Tyson and Paul Winfield, has an Oscar-

Two black icons at work in *Lady Sings the Blues*. (Courtesy of Paramount Pictures.)

nominated script by Lonnie Elder III and a wonderful performance by young Kevin Hooks.

- Ossie Davis directs *Black Girl*, with a script by J. E. Franklin adapted from her play. Cinerama distributed and Brock Peters and Leslie Uggams starred.

- *Shaft's Big Score*, directed by Gordon Parks Sr., isn't as much fun as the original. After intense negotiations, Roundtree is paid $50,000 to reprise his role.

- *Come Back Charleston Blue*, the sequel to *Cotton Comes to Harlem*, is directed by black TV director Mark Warren.

- *Blacula*, a black Dracula flick from AIP, stars William Marshall and is directed by Bill Crain, who'd go on to become black horror's shlocky auteur.

- *Across 110th Street*, with Yaphet Kotto, Anthony Quinn, and Antonio Fargas, is a little gem about black crooks stealing Mafia money. Rich in hypocrisy and characterization, it examines the complexities of loyalty in a shifting urban environment.

- Maya Angelou scripts the Diana Sands vehicle *Georgia, Georgia*. This tale of a tortured singer's relationship with her white audience and her mother was shot in Europe (Cinerama). While Hollywood was discovering the black audience, over at UCLA, a group of film students was exploring black film aesthetics. Among the historically important black indies who came out of this exploratory environment were Larry Clark, Ben Caldwell, Haile Gerima, and Charles Burnett.

Slaughter (AIP) with Jim Brown is the ex-football star's attempt to create a *Shaft*-like vehicle. The character ended up in two more movies but never made the impact of Roundtree's detective. Gloria Hendry, who was the love interest in a slew of blaxploitation films, is Slaughter's woman here.

Melinda (MGM) has Calvin Lockhart, Vonetta McGee, and a screenplay by Lonnie Elder III, yet this slightly kinky melodrama is little remembered.

1973

Variety estimates that 35 percent of the audiences for recent blockbusters *The Godfather* and *The Exorcist* are black.

Bruce Lee stars in his breakthrough film *Enter the Dragon,* ably supported by black martial artist Jim Kelly. Kelly's prominent role speaks to the producer's knowledge of African-American enthusiasm for martial arts films.

To Find an Image: Black Films from Uncle Tom to Superfly (Bobbs-Merrill) by James P. Murray is one of the first book-length views of black film by a black author. Murray articulated the hopes of many when he wrote, "The three goals of Black cinema are: correction of white distortions, the reflection of Black reality, and [as a propagandizing tool] the creation of a positive image."

Black film historian Pearl Bowser's "The Boom Is Really an Echo" in *Black Creation* magazine introduces many to the hectic world of race movies between the wars. Bowser's lectures and archival efforts bring Oscar Micheaux, Jr.'s prolific career to the attention of a new generation.

Playwright Richard Wesley's essay "Which Way Black Film" makes several interesting points: he identifies the black-directed *Shaft, Cotton Comes to Harlem*, and *Superfly* as having black style; he predicts the end of black action-thriller films because they're so predictable; he identifies *Sounder* and *Nothing But a Man* as the future of black film.

The family comedy *Five on the Black Hand Side* is directed by Oscar Williams. The screenplay is by Charles Russell from his play. Actor Brock Peters serves as a co-producer. Glynn Turman, Clarice Taylor, and Virginia Capers star.

The Harder They Come is one of the first of a new cultural phenomenon, the midnight cult movie supported by hipster audiences. Shot in Jamaica and starring singer Jimmy Cliff, this feature was instrumental in developing a multiracial following for reggae music.

Pam Grier's reign as blaxploitation sex symbol begins with her title role in *Coffy*. The ad tag line is, "She is the 'Godmother' of them all." The buxom actress goes on to top line with *Foxy Brown*, *Sheba Baby*, and *Friday Foster*. Of *Foxy Brown* (AIP) *Variety* wrote, "Tasteful finale has (Pam) Grier delivering [villain's] private parts in a pickle jar to white ring leader (Kathryn) Loder, before driving off with neighborhood vigilante leader . . ." Grier would become a cult figure who was even embraced by many feminists for her ball-breaking action flicks. She remains one of the few women of any color in American film history who had vehicles developed for her that emphasized not just her physical beauty, but also her ability to take retribution on men who challenged her.

St. Clair Bourne's documentary *Let the Church Say Amen!* brings a Northern black sensibility to bear on a rich black Southern obsession, the Baptist church.

The documentary *Save the Children*, shot at the Chicago Black Expo, is directed by Stan Lathan and produced and written by Matt Robinson. The talent gathered includes the Jackson Five, Marvin Gaye, Nancy Wilson, Curtis Mayfield, Gladys Knight & the Pips, and Roberta Flack.

The Spook Who Sat By the Door is directed by Ivan Dixon. Sam Greenlee adapts the film from his novel about a black CIA operative who uses his training to school a team of revolutionary youths. *Variety* called

Fred Williamson, blaxploitation king, doin' his thang. (Courtesy of Orion Home Video.)

the film "a typical blaxploitationer" with "little gore but lotsa racist and revolutionary blather."

- *Black Caesar* and the follow-up, *Hell Up in Harlem*, both starring Fred Williamson and written and directed by shlockmaster Larry Cohen, are loosely based on the mystique of Harlem drug lord Nicky Barnes. *Black Caesar* features an amazing James Brown score, including the classic "The Payback."

- With Williamson starring in *The Legend of Nigger Charley,* the "N" word goes aboveground.

- *Shaft in Africa* (MGM), shot in Africa and France, is highlighted by Vonetta McGee's presence as an African princess.

- In *Superfly T.N.T.*, directed by star Ron O'Neal, the drug dealer turns good guy while living in Europe. The script was by a then-struggling author named Alex Haley.

- *Toms, Coons, Mulattoes, Mammies & Bucks: An Interpretative History of Blacks in American Film* (Viking), by Donald Bogle, is published.

Bogle's reinterpretation of blacks in Hollywood invested these actors and actresses with a dignity heretofore denied by most historians.

Tamara Dobson mounts a short-lived challenge to Pam Grier with the action flick *Cleopatra Jones* (Warner Bros.). Co-written and co-produced by Max Julien, the film gets decent reviews and has Shelley Winters as Dobson's worthy adversary. Dobson, as a model turned undercover cop, does well enough to spawn a sequel.

In *Gordon's War* a group of Vietnam vets comes back to Harlem to take on drug dealers. Paul Winfield brings some weight to the title role under Ossie Davis's direction.

Wattstax is a documentary of a Stax Records music festival at the L.A. Coliseum with performances by Isaac Hayes, the Staple Singers, the Bar-Kays, Richard Pryor (telling stories in a bar), and the Reverend Jesse "I Am Somebody" Jackson.

Raymond St. Jacques stars in, directs, and raises the funding for *Book of Numbers*, which also stars singer Freda Payne and young actor Philip Michael Thomas. This look at black Depression era con men deserved more attention.

The Bar-Kays, a Memphis-based funk band, at the premiere of *Wattstax* at the Criterion Theater in New York's Times Square. (Courtesty of Stax Records.)

1974

- *Blazing Saddles*, a great Mel Brooks comedy, stars Cleavon Little as a black sheriff in the old West. Much of the sharp racial humor was contributed by co-screenwriter Richard Pryor.

- Jim Kelly stars in one of the few explicitly black kung fu flicks, *Black Belt Jones* (Warner Bros.).

- Psychologist Alvin Poussaint, later a consultant to "The Cosby Show," writes a damning antiblaxploitation essay in February's *Psychology Today*.

- In *Three the Hard Way*, a plot to drop a sickle cell anemia poison in the water supplies of big cities is foiled by Jim Brown, Fred Williamson, and Jim Kelly. Gordon Parks Jr. directed.

- Gordon Parks Jr. is also behind the camera for *Thomasine and Bushrod*, a Western meets romantic comedy that starred blaxploitation's first couple, Max Julien and Vonetta McGee.

- Julien also writes the script for *The Black 6* which stars six football players—Gene Washington, Lem Barney, Willie Lanier, Carl Eller, Mercury Morris, and "Mean" Joe Greene as bikers. Greene's best acting could be found in a popular Coke commercial.

- Gordon Parks Sr. directs *The Super Cops*, an urban policer about two heroic white men, the first nonblack studio film helmed by an African-American.

- *Claudine* is the kind of picture that black folks hoped blaxploitation would lead to. The love affair between James Earl Jones's garbage man and Diahann Carroll's welfare mother had plenty of heart and soul. Gladys Knight & the Pips contributed the great title song "On and On."

- In AIP's continuing search for black dollars it makes *Abby*, a black *Exorcist* directed by Bill Girdler with Carol Speed in the title role.

Glynn Turman (left)
and Lawrence
Hilton-Jacobs
(middle) brought
the early sixties to
life in *Cooley High*.
(Courtesy of
American
International
Pictures.)

Black writer-producer Matt Robinson creates *Amazing Grace*, directed
by Stan Lathan, as a vehicle for seventysomething chitlin' circuit comedian Moms Mabley. Also in the cast are the venerable Butterfly
McQueen, Slappy White, and Stepin Fetchit.

1975

Michael Schultz directs *Cooley High* from Eric Monte's autobiographical
script set in early sixties Chicago. Though often compared to *American
Graffiti*, this film has a pulse and character of its own. Glynn Turman and
Lawrence Hilton-Jacobs share the spotlight with the first score to tap
Motown music's nostalgia value. This may be the most unabashedly loved
black film of all-time. Despite good reviews and box office, Monte doesn't
have another movie script produced. But, by again drawing on his Chicago
childhood, he helps create the hit sitcom "Good Times" for Norman Lear.

Black films generate black film books: black writer Lindsay Patterson
compiles *Black Films and Film-makers: A Comprehensive Anthology from
Stereotype to Super-Hero* (Dodd, Mead) and Daniel Leab writes *From
Sambo to Superspade: The Black Experience in Motion Pictures*
(Houghton Mifflin).

Berry Gordy directs *Mahogany*, a gaudy potboiler about a model, played breathlessly by Diana Ross, who leaves her politically active boyfriend (Billy Dee Williams) to pursue a career in Europe under the guidance of a decadent photographer (Anthony Perkins). Ross designed the garish outfits which, along with Gordy's direction, gave the entire project the feel of an expensive vanity project. Gordy's tag line for the movie was right out of a Supremes' song, "Success means nothing if you have no one to share it with."

Aaron Loves Angela is an at times refreshing look at love across ethnic lines as black Aaron (Kevin Hooks) falls for a Puerto Rican girl (Irene Cara). This modest little film was Gordon Parks Jr.'s last. He perished in a 1979 plane crash in Africa at age forty-four.

Cornbread, Earl and Me is a drama with an engaging mix of basketball, coming-of-age, and crime that has an excellent cast: Larry Fishburne, Rosalind Cash, Madge Sinclair, Bernie Casey, Moses Gunn, and basketball star Jamal Wilkes.

Mandingo is a trashy southern gothic that uses interracial sex as its steamy selling point. White actor Perry King gets to bed down blaxploitation queen Brenda Sykes, though the main event is boxer Ken Norton and white southern belle Susan George. After all his hard work, Norton gets dumped in a vat of steaming water. *Mandingo* performed so well that Norton returned for the sequel, *Drum*.

Haile Gerima's *Harvest: 3,000 Years* is one of the first black indie films to gain significant critical attention. Gerima, who shot the film in Ethiopia and would teach at Howard University, becomes an icon of the still underground, anti-imperialist, non-Hollywood black film movement.

Sidney Poitier's *Let's Do It Again*, sort of a sequel to *Uptown Saturday Night*, reunites Poitier, Bill Cosby, and writer Richard Wesley. The genial comedy is the highest-grossing black film of the seventies.

Radical animator Ralph Bakshi caricatures black culture in *Coonskin*. Even using the voices of Barry White and Scatman Crothers couldn't suppress criticism of the film's exaggerated depictions of street life.

1976

Sparkle is a celebration of black girl groups written by Joel Schumacher, who for several years was Hollywood's resident "black" screenwriter. It has an incredible R & B score by Curtis Mayfield and an amazing cast of young actors (Irene Cara, Philip Michael Thomas, Dorian Harewood, Lonette McKee). En Vogue later covered "Givin' Him Something He Can Feel" from the score. In an oddity Irene Cara and Lonette McKee sang the songs in the film, but not for the soundtrack album for which Aretha Franklin recorded all of Mayfield's material.

Young director John Badham, later to go on to big-budget successes, cuts his feature teeth on *The Bingo Long Traveling All-Stars and Motor Kings*. This saga of a thirties barnstorming black baseball team stars Billy Dee Williams, James Earl Jones, and Richard Pryor. Badham had directed Williams previously in a made-for-TV movie about Scott Joplin. Pryor, as he did throughout this period, stole the movie; the irony of Pryor's film career is that he did his best work not as a star but as the second banana to straight men like Williams.

The black Delta Sigma Theta sorority finances *Countdown to Kusini*, a well-intentioned thriller shot in Lagos, Nigeria, about a pianist ("Mission Impossible" star Greg Morris) who gets caught up in a liberation struggle. The film lost its shirt and Ossie Davis, who hadn't had a hit since *Cotton Comes to Harlem*, doesn't direct another feature after this.

The River Niger, based on Joseph Walker's hit Negro Ensemble Company play, is a major disappointment. Under the direction of East Indian director Krishna Shah, an exceptional black cast (James Earl Jones, Louis Gossett Jr., Cicely Tyson, Glynn Turman) is wasted. Nice score by War.

Rocky, written by and starring Sylvester Stallone, shows Hollywood that the black action crowd can be attracted by films with prominent black second bananas, such as this film's Apollo Creed played by Carl Weathers. This discovery is a crucial death blow to the already sagging blaxploitation genre. The film wins the Academy Award for best picture.

James Baldwin publishes *The Devil Finds Work*, a book of film memories and criticism that's memorable for its takes on Bette Davis and *The Exorcist*.

Gordon Parks Sr. directs *Leadbelly* for Paramount. This beautiful-looking biography of the great folksinger dies at the box office and begins the yet-to-be-turned-around Hollywood truism that "Black period films don't make money."

Bill Crain takes a final stab at the horror genre with *Dr. Black and Mr. Hyde*. Bernie Casey portrays the mixed-up doctor in this one, also known as *The Watts Monster* (Someone must organize the Bill Crain black horror festival!)

Richard Pryor's crossover power is confirmed by his supporting role in the Gene Wilder vehicle *Silver Streak*. His entry into the film halfway through infuses the story with energy and fun. Though Pryor and Wilder have obvious chemistry, it's the black comic's skills that make everything work.

In *Ceddo*, Ousmane Sembène looks at the ideological struggle between Muslims and those who believe in ancient African myths (aka *Ceddos*) in a village. The kidnapping of a Muslim princess by a *Ceddo* brings this simmering struggle to the fore.

Haile Gerima's *Bush Mama* is the story of a welfare mother trying to survive against structural racism in Los Angeles. Through her daughter she finds her inspiring solution. For Gerima the personal is always controlled by larger political forces.

Michael Schultz's *Car Wash* wins two awards at Cannes, making it the first film by a black director accepted at a major international competition. The Universal-distributed film was widely hailed in Europe, but treated as just another blaxploitation flick in the United States. Richard Pryor's star turn as a slick preacher drew raves, while Norman Whitfield's wall-to-wall funk score generated massive hits for Rose Royce. Bill Duke plays Abdullah, the quintessential angry black nationalist without a cause, while Franklin Ajaye is funny as a car washer in love.

1977

Charles Burnett's *Killer of Sheep* is hailed as a landmark by critics in the United States and Europe.

Larry Clark's *Passing Through* uses a generic mystery framework to craft a search for the roots of black musical creativity. Papa Harris is a master jazzman and Warmack, the protagonist, wanders the streets of Los Angeles seeking this man and his sounds. The film is a very ambitious attempt to capture the texture of jazz in visual terms.

Warrington Hudlin's *Street Corner Stories*, a ninety-minute cinema vérité student film about working-class black men who gather mornings at a New Haven diner to exchange philosophies, is a festival favorite and introduces this Yale grad to the film world at large.

Slow Fade to Black: The Negro in American Film, 1900-1942 (Oxford University Press) by Morgan State University professor Thomas Cripps is an exhaustive history of black employment and abuse at all levels of American moviemaking before World War II.

Muhammad Ali plays himself in the adaptation of his autobiography *The Greatest*. Now the film is best remembered for its oft-covered title song, "The Greatest Love of All."

Universal gives Richard Pryor a nonexclusive deal that guarantees him $3 million for four years as a performer-writer. He signs a similar deal with Warner Bros. in the same year. Pryor begins a short-lived NBC variety show in September that is at times quite brilliant. However, Pryor and the network censors become mortal enemies and the show ends after only six episodes.

1978

The Black Filmmaker Foundation is founded by Warrington Hudlin, scholar George Cunningham, and businessman Al Emhart. The initial $10,000 in seed money was provided by the National Endowment for the Arts, which was then matched by $10,000 from the Ford Foundation.

Warrington Hudlin, independent filmmaker and co-founder of the Black Filmmaker Foundation.

Richard Pryor, the biggest black movie star of the seventies. (Courtesy of Partree.)

- Julie Dash's *Four Women* is a short based on the Nina Simone song that through its use of color and movement attempts to replicate visually the song's somber strength. Though it is a short film, it introduces visual themes that would recur in Dash's later narrative work.

- Bill Cosby and Richard Pryor, two of the greatest black comedians of all time, work together in the silliest of four vignettes that make up Neil Simon's *California Suite*. As two doctors on vacation who end up at each other's throats, neither man is at the top of his game.

- *The Wiz* signals the end of Hollywood's interest in making big-budget black films (at least for the time being). This Sidney Lumet–directed $30 million flop was the biggest-budgeted musical of all time. Universal's favorite black screenwriter Joel Schumacher adapted *The Wiz*, which was a black adaptation of *The Wizard of Oz*. Quincy Jones was one of the few African-Americans with power behind the scenes. Diana Ross was miscast as Dorothy, while most of the other players, including Richard Pryor and Michael Jackson, were ineffectual in their roles. Only vets Nipsey Russell and Lena Horne commanded the screen. A great-looking, lethargic work.

- Stan Shaw is impressive as a macho soldier in *The Boys in Company C.*

1979

- *Richard Pryor Live in Concert* is the first film to capture the full range of his comic gift. This is a genius work, full of insight into human nature, wonderful acting as Pryor mines the behavior of children and inanimate objects, and just one funny comment after another. Nothing else, not even his other two concert films, matches his work in this independently distributed documentary.

- Michael Schultz directs a badly conceived, big-budget musical based on the Beatles' *Sgt. Pepper's Lonely Hearts Club Band*. The Bee Gees and Peter Frampton both had their careers destroyed by the film and Schultz wasn't helped by it either. The best moments were a Steve Martin cameo performing "Maxwell's Silver Hammer," an inspired "Got to Get You into My Life" by Earth Wind and Fire, and Billy Preston doing "Get Back."

- Julius "Dr. J" Erving proves he's no thespian in *The Fish that Saved Pittsburgh*, a film about astrology and basketball directed by Gilbert Moses.

- Indie film supporter Oliver Franklin gets the NEA and Sun Oil Company to finance a five-city tour of black filmmakers that includes Haile Gerima, Charles Burnett, Warrington Hudlin, and Carol Mindy Lawrence.

- The BFF inaugurates a Filmmobile that presents the work of eighteen black and Latino filmmakers in parks around New York. That fall the foundation has screenings of work by indie filmmakers in unusual locations such as discos. One successful screening is held in Othello's disco on Eighth Avenue where Charles Lane's 1976 Chaplinesque silent comedy, *A Place In Time,* shot in black and white, is shown.

- Teenager Larry Fishburne and veteran Albert Hall turn in stellar performances in Francis Ford Coppola's *Apocalypse Now*.

1980

- Richard Pryor and Gene Wilder star in the Sidney Poitier—directed *Stir Crazy*, which earns over $100 million in revenues. This is the first film by a black director to make that much at the box office. Sadly, at just this moment Pryor burns over half his body while freebasing cocaine. Though there are still many big paychecks on the horizon, Pryor is never quite the same.

- Who says blaxploitation died in '75? Jamaa Fanaka's *Penitentiary* is a whacked-out, jailhouse version of *Rocky,* with Leon Isaac Kennedy quite fun as Too Sweet, our reluctant hero. The film made much money and spawned two sequels.

- Sidney Poitier writes his autobiography, *This Life*, in which he talks about the pressures he felt as black film's solo star in the sixties and his relief at the rise of other stars in the seventies.

- The BFF sponsors a five-day conference of Black Independent Filmmakers at City University of New York's midtown campus. There are panels during the day and screenings at night. Representatives from film festivals in Amsterdam and Paris attend. This will result in screenings of black films in Paris in 1980 and in Amsterdam in March 1981. One of the conference's last-minute registrants is Spike Lee.

- The BFF also establishes a black film distribution service that serves as a clearinghouse for those interested in renting black films. It is the first time many of these films are made accessible to the community.

- Charles Burnett, Charles Lane, Michelle Parkinson, and Warrington Hudlin attend the 1980 Berlin Film Festival.

1981

- Thom Mount, vice president of production at Universal, tells *Black Enterprise*: "Black films are not capable of making money. There's only one actor who's bankable, Richard Pryor, and one actress, Diana Ross, and we have Pryor under contract." Pryor stars in Universal's *Bustin' Loose* with Cicely Tyson. Though Oz Scott is listed as director, Michael Schultz supervised extensive reshoots. Black film vet Williams Greaves executive produced. Released after Pryor's infamous freebase accident, the film has several unintentional laughs involving a child who enjoys arson. According to the NAACP Image Award committee, Tyson was the only black actress with a major role in a feature this year.

In adapting E. L. Doctorow's *Ragtime*, Academy Award—winning director Miloš Forman emphasizes the role of the black militant Coalhouse Walker. Though Howard Rollins plays him with less anger than the book indicates, the young actor still earns a best supporting actor nomination. Debbie Allen as Walker's wife and Moses Gunn as Booker T. Washington also have significant roles.

Denzel Washington has his first starring role in the Michael Schultz—directed comedy *Carbon Copy*. Washington is miscast as the unknown son of a white man played by George Segal.

In the third and fourth quarters of this year, of 13,043 male actors working, only 832 are black males and only 1.9 percent had lead roles. Of 5,710 female actresses working, only 335 are black women and only 1.8 percent had lead roles. Of 5,700 writers in the Guild West, only 7 are black. Of 240 films, only 12 had black leads.

Jim Kelly sells real estate and gives tennis lessons to make ends meet. He tells *Black Enterprise*, "White America is not quite ready for black heroes."

A festival of black indie films is held in Chicago. This successful promotion inspires the Windy City's long-running Black Light film festival.

1982

Kathleen Collins's *Losing Ground* is, on one level, a look at the life of a black female university professor much like herself. But Collins's approach is post-mod, not naturalistic, and shows us the making of the film as well as the film itself. At 86 minutes it is the first feature-length work by an African-American woman.

Louis Gossett Jr. wins the supporting actor Oscar for his role in *An Officer and a Gentleman*. Gossett's work was so strong that the demanding black drill instructor became a cinematic cliché of the decade.

After emerging on "Saturday Night Live" as the show's first black star, Eddie Murphy makes a charismatic screen debut in *48 HRS.* opposite Nick Nolte. Funny, cynical, and handsome, Murphy is an instant movie star.

Richard Pryor Live on the Sunset Strip is his second concert film and, while lacking the sustained brilliance of the first, is still often sidesplitting. The centerpiece is a long section on the fire in which Pryor humorously and graphically describes his freebasing accident. Highlights include impersonations of Jim Brown and a talking freebase pipe.

Hanky Panky is the first film Sidney Poitier directs that he doesn't appear in. This vehicle for the husband-and-wife team of Gene Wilder and Gilda Radner is a bomb.

In *Rocky III* Carl Weathers's Apollo Creed helps Rocky train to fight the brutal black buck Clubber Lang, embodied by ex-bodyguard Mr. T. Weathers brings Sly Stallone to a black gym where he gets rhythm. Stallone's script shrewdly exploits the class differences between the more refined Weathers and the roughneck Mr. T.

Two events showcase African-American indie filmmakers in London, one held at the National Film Theatre and the other sponsored by the British Commonwealth Institute.

White indie director George Nierenberg makes *Say Amen, Somebody*, a moving documentary about the world of gospel music that centers around 83-year-old gospel creator Thomas Dorsey and 78-year-old Willie Mae Ford Smith. The role of women in the black church is the film's smart subtext.

White filmmaker Charlie Ahearn's *Wild Style* is the first realistic depiction of the emerging hip-hop culture. Old-school rapper Busy Bee and painter-screenmaker Fab Five Freddie add flavor to this documentary-style feature.

Eddie Murphy, one of
the eighties' biggest
movies stars–period.
(Courtesy of
Paramount Pictures.)

1983

- Julie Dash's *Illusions* is an assured indie short about a smart black woman passing for white at a Hollywood studio during World War II. Lonette McKee stars in this low-budget yet evocative work that illuminates the subversive strength of black women in a racist culture. The film would later be named BFF Film of the Decade by a panel of judges.

- Alfre Woodard is given a supporting actress Oscar nomination for her role as a maid in Martin Ritt's gentle *Cross Creek*.

- Columbia announces Richard Pryor has been given $40 million to make films under his Indigo Films banner. But little comes of the deal and Pryor eventually gives the money back.

- In July, Pryor and Eddie Murphy share the cover of *People* magazine.

- D'Urville Martin, Fred Williamson's partner in Po Boy Productions, tells *Players* magazine, "Black critics have been criminal in their treatment of black films and black filmmakers—now they're out of work."

- Harvard undergrad Reginald Hudlin directs a well-received short about a son who sneaks out to a party against his father's wishes. It's titled *House Party*.

- Mr. T. toplines the disjointed comedy *D.C. Cab*, which is directed and written by Joel Schumacher. Black producer Topper Carew conceived the original story. Its existence is testimony to that inexplicable period of Mr. T mania.

■ Spike Lee does a spec video of Grandmaster Flash and the Furious Five's "White Lines" that Sugarhill turns down. Larry Fishburne plays the villainous protagonist.

■ *Flashdance* introduces the feature film as long-form video, hastens the burnout of break dancing, and introduces Jennifer Beals, one of the many biracial women to become sex symbols in the coming years.

■ Eddie Murphy proves *48 HRS.* was no fluke with a great comic performance in *Trading Places.* The film earns $90 million and it is suddenly clear that Hollywood can now replace Pryor with Murphy just as Pryor eventually replaced Poitier.

■ A twelve-nation tour of African-American indie films is financed by the United States Information Agency (which is rumored to be cozy with the CIA).

■ Before his sitcom success, Bill Cosby directed, wrote, and produced a concert film titled *Bill Cosby, Himself,* which doesn't simply reveal his ample comic skills, but also suggests that under his charming exterior is a tough, demanding man.

1984

■ *Purple Rain* takes its cult star Prince, a musically ambitious, sexually daring, and racially ambiguous musician, and elevates him to superstardom. Set in Minneapolis, this high-energy musical percolates with his brilliant productions of songs from his *Purple Rain* album as well as choice cuts from The Time led by Morris Day. In his casually androgynous way, Prince is charismatic. The surprise of the film is how funny a duo Day and side-kick-valet Jerome Benton prove to be.

■ White indie filmmaker John Sayles makes *The Brother from Another Planet.* Shot in Harlem by Ernest Dickerson (his first feature) and starring Joe Morton, the film didn't have the flavor a black filmmaker can provide, but compared to the way many whites have depicted black life, Sayles showed great imagination and his usual writing skill. Sayles contacted the BFF for suggestions in hiring the crew for *Brother*.

- Hollywood checks in with *Beat Street*, one of several awful rap-breakdance flicks. Harry Belafonte is one of the producers and Stan Lathan directs. Pioneering boho Rae Dawn Chong plays the love interest. The highlight is a powerful rap by Grand Master Melle Mel near the film's end called "Beat Street Breakdown."

- Eddie Murphy makes his first cinematic mistake in the bad Dudley Moore vehicle *Best Defense*. But Murphy's part is so small—he doesn't even appear with Moore in a scene—that his fans thankfully ignore the film.

- Francis Ford Coppola's *The Cotton Club* overplays unsympathetic white gangsters and underplays interesting black entertainers in his pulpy look at the famous twenties Harlem hangout. Gregory Hines's dancer and Lonette McKee's singer, who passes for white, are an engaging couple. Larry Fishburne, as the real Harlem kingpin Bumpy Jones, has a couple of tasty moments.

- With *The Killing Floor*, actor Bill Duke makes his directing debut. This indie project depicts the conflicts between black and white workers in the Chicago stockyards in the thirties. This is a tough, hard-hitting film that generated much work for Duke as a television director, though his feature break wouldn't occur until the black new wave of the late eighties. Duke's most passionate behind-the-camera work to date.

- *A Soldier's Story* has a screenplay by Charles Fuller based on his Pulitzer Prize–winning play. Norman Jewison (*In the Heat of the Night*) again turns in sensitive direction of a black story set in the South. The cast is thick with talent—Howard Rollins, Denzel Washington, Adolph Caesar, Art Evans, and, in a small part, Robert Townsend.

- Euzhan Palcy directs *Sugar Cane Alley*, the coming-of-age story of a precocious eight-year-old boy growing up on the French-speaking island of Martinique in 1930: a supple, insightful picture of class and color conflicts within this black community. It is a confident debut for one of the few women of color to get a film released theatrically in the United States.

1985

Black buddies abound: Gregory Hines plays second fiddle to Mikhail Baryshnikov in *White Nights*, while Louis Gossett Jr., coming off his Oscar win, plays an androgynous alien opposite Dennis Quaid in *Enemy Mine*.

Krush Groove captures vintage performances by Run-D.M.C., the Fat Boys, Kurtis Blow, and wonderful cameos by L. L. Cool J and Dr. Jeckyll and Mr. Hyde. It even has a set made up to look like the crucial hip-hop hang out, the Bronx's Disco Fever. But despite being based loosely on the life of hip-hop promoter Russell Simmons, the film is more Hollywood than hip-hop. A slew of significant black creative talent was behind the scenes—director Michael Schultz, cinematographer Ernest Dickerson, producer Doug McHenry—but this never became the *Cooley High* of rap many hoped. *Krush Groove* is the highest-grossing film of the weekend, earning $3 million at 515 theaters, but its opening in New York is marred by violence, though it still made $1 million in the city. This combination of opening-weekend box office success and opening-weekend violence will be seen again and again with black youth films.

Alice Walker's *The Color Purple* (Warner/Amblin) is a poetic and controversial bestseller about the struggle of a black woman in the

Run-D.M.C. performs "King of Rock" in Krush Groove. (Courtesy of Warner Bros.)

Michael Schulz, for a long time Hollywood's only prominent black director. (Courtesy of Warner Bros.)

Depression-era south. Some black men complained about male bashing but producer Quincy Jones and director Steven Spielberg loved it and turned Walker's wonderfully written novel into a glossy tearjerker. In one fell swoop they made Whoopi Goldberg an international star and talk-show queen Oprah Winfrey into an actress. The film made $94 million.

Though Michael Schultz was listed as director, the film's title, *Berry Gordy's The Last Dragon*, reveals who had the power on the set of this black martial arts fantasy. Vanity was the heroine of this minor hit. A planned sequel never came to pass.

Grace Jones is the female love interest of villain Christopher Walken in the Bond film *A View to a Kill*.

1986

Richard Pryor directs *Jo Jo Dancer, Your Life Is Calling*, a flawed yet ambitious autobiographical film. Pryor's start as a young comic at a strip club with Paula Kelly, Art Evans, and Billy Eckstine beautifully evokes the conditions on the chitlin' circuit.

Forest Whitaker has only one scene in *The Color of Money*. But as a pool shark who hustles Paul Newman, Whitaker projects the charming yet lethal qualities that quickly made him one of film's most respected character actors.

- More buddy work: Gregory Hines is a winning co-star to Billy Crystal in the fun cops-and-robbers flick *Running Scared*.

- Louis Gossett Jr. gets to flex his macho instincts as a badass fighter pilot in *Iron Eagle*, which spawns two sequels.

- At a press conference for the desultory comedy/special effects film *The Golden Child*, Eddie Murphy uses the phrase "black pack" to describe his friendship with Arsenio Hall, Robert Townsend, Keenen Ivory Wayans, and Paul Mooney.

- *Jumpin' Jack Flash* is the best of several bad post–*Color Purple* comedies starring Whoopi Goldberg.

- *Under the Cherry Moon*, starring and directed by Prince, is a real bad movie. Playing a fey French Riviera gigolo, Prince indulges his worst acting and story instincts, even underutilizing his own often superb music. This flick lost the Minneapolis native tons of fans.

- *Soul Man* with Rae Dawn Chong enrages a lot of black folks but does excellent business. In the film, C. Thomas Howell wears blackface makeup to attend law school on a minority scholarship. It must have been a very effective performance since Chong and Howell got married, albeit briefly, after the production.

- Spike Lee's *She's Gotta Have It* opens in New York City, and the world of black film changes forever.

Screening invitation for She's Gotta Have It. Courtesy of Nelson George.

FORT GREENE DREAMS

I was still living in Queens in the mid-eighties when I tuned in to PBS one night and saw Spike Lee's *Joe's Bed-Stuy Barbershop: We Cut Heads*. I was immediately homesick. Queens was a room I slept in but it wasn't my home. I was a Brooklyn boy to my core. Circumstance (going to St. John's University) and money (my room-mate had cash and I didn't) had landed me in a foreign borough. Spike's student Academy Award–winning short was filled with lov-ing depictions of brownstones, projects, and elevated subways that touched a part of me in a way Queen's cute two-story homes and backyards never could. My heart was already yearning for reunion, and Spike's wonderful first effort about barbershops and numbers running just intensified the feelings.

Unfortunately, from graduation in 1979 to the spring of 1984, cash was in short supply. I'd successfully made the entry into the music journalism business—as *Record World*'s black music editor in 1981 and to the same position at *Billboard* in 1982—but the checks were small and my postcollege debts large. With freelance work from various fanzines, slick magazines, and the occasional record company artist bio, I was getting by when my luck changed. In the spring of 1983, Dell Books contacted me about doing a quickie paperback biography of Michael Jackson. I was the publisher's sec-ond choice but, hey, I was in no position to be picky.

After the initial success of *Thriller* and his appearance on the "Motown 25" television special, Jackson had begun to move into his reclusive mode. I'd met him a couple of times in my days as a rookie critic but didn't have anything substantial on him. What I did have was a slew of interviews with Jermaine, LaToya, father Joe, mother Katherine, Quincy Jones, sundry ex-Motowners and *Thriller* sidemen. With help from journalist friends, I stitched together a fan's guide to the Jackson family saga that, due to my editor's unkind cuts, was softer than I might have liked. Nevertheless, published in January 1984 just after Michael was burned shooting a Pepsi commercial in Los Angeles and right before his huge party in New York's American Museum of Natural

History, *The Michael Jackson Story* was an immediate bestseller, the first of many to appear that year on The Gloved One. This event is important to this current tale for two reasons: I had the cash to move back to Brooklyn, and it was money made on that biography that I'd later invest in *She's Gotta Have It*.

I ended up in a new (for me) Brooklyn neighborhood, Fort Greene. Located just to the right of downtown Brooklyn and to the left of Bedford-Stuyvesant, Fort Greene was a place I remembered for its huge public-housing project and notorious gang initiations held in Fort Greene, aka Washington, Park (captured in the blaxploitation flick *The Education of Sonny Carson*, which I saw at a marijuana-filled Times Square theater). As a teen I'd avoided it at all costs.

But by 1984 Fort Greene's gang days were a memory and it was well on its way to a new image as a cultural center of sorts. Its restored brownstones held some of New York's best real estate bargains. Jazz musicians like Wynton and Branford Marsalis had already settled there, as had many actors, including Larry Fishburne and Wesley Snipes, and a great many young artists of every stripe. There has always been a strong white art contingent because Pratt Institute is located in Fort Greene's eastern end. The demarcation of Fort Greene's western end is provided by the park, a lush, hilly space that accommodates weekend soccer matches, several tennis courts, more pit bulls than you can shake a chain at, and a tall tower that is visible for miles around (at its base Spike shot *She's Gotta Have It*'s one color sequence).

Between these two borders I found a sense of community that I hadn't known since my childhood in the 'Ville. There were good restaurants like Cino's and Two Steps Down and fun hangouts such as Junior's Deli just across Flatbush Avenue. Most important there were all these artists around. Sometimes at night I'd walk the streets and literally feel the creative buzz in the air. It made me want to rush home and get busy writing myself. After scrambling to make ends meet in Queens I was excited to be in such a stimulating place. To be young and black and working at my craft in Fort Greene was a genuine high. And it wasn't too long before the rest of the world started paying attention to Fort Greene because of its native son and de facto mayor, Shelton "Spike" Lee.

The brownstone duplex I settled in turned out to be a block and a half from Spike's joint. At that time the gap between the more upwardly mobile part of Fort Greene and its working-class residents was defined by the difference between De Kalb and Myrtle avenues. De Kalb had the cool restaurants and Perry's, a great little grocery store. Two blocks to the north was Myrtle, which bordered on the projects and had tons of fast food spots and clusters of drug dealers even before crack arrived.

I lived on Willoughby, the street between De Kalb and Myrtle that ran right into the park. Spike lived across Myrtle on Adelphi in a cluttered two-room hovel dominated by an editing board, a bed, a stereo, and an early Michael Jordan poster. In piles along the floor and in shelves were tapes, records, papers, photographs, you name it. Now when folks complain that Spike's films seem scattered and stuffed with too many themes, I often reflect on that apartment. Just as with his best work, there was ambition manifest in that room that held the seeming chaos together.

Much has been written over the years about *She's Gotta Have It*. All I can do is make you see the movie as how I saw it then. First and foremost I recall how damn fresh it felt to me. Nola Darling, while a little one-note as a character, hit a real deep note with me. Tracy Camilla Johns's performance captured the essence of many of the free-spirited, artsy women who populated Fort Greene. Today we'd call Nola a boho in good standing. Back in 1986 there was no cutesy designation for her blend of sexual freedom, artistic interest, and unconventional worldview.

Greer Childs's buppie, Mars Blackmon's b-boy, and Jamie Overstreet's sober everyman were all perfectly on the mark. Their bickering Thanksgiving dinner is one of the funniest and most truthful scenes involving brothers I've ever seen. Class and age differences, as well as sexual competitiveness, are all deftly captured by dialogue, body language, and costumes. The combination of these men, along with Nola and Opal Gilstrap, tapped some of the complexity of my generation, what was new and funny, unfocused and old-fashioned about us, better than any film before or since. Spike and I were both twenty-eight in 1985. At some point while I was watching the film in his crowded little space, I realized I'd moved around the corner from one of the key artists of my generation.

I made it my business to be an ardent advocate for Spike, and hooked him up with a number of music industry figures who might be interested in investment in the film or getting involved in the soundtrack. Most of them fronted on Spike. Some were turned off by the fact that the film was in black and white. A few hated his father's score. (I don't know if they told Spike that, but they definitely told me.) What bothered me was the lack of imagination displayed by these black folks with cash. Black indie films were an abstraction to them and Spike's film, though they could see it, still seemed unreal to them. The film couldn't work, they felt, because Hollywood hadn't done it. Instead of being excited by being in on a new movement, they feared losing money on a small investment. Well, I believed and gave Spike a couple of thousand of my hard-earned Michael Jackson dollars. It was a scary thing to do, but Spike inspired confidence.

As you might discern from the production diary published as *Spike Lee's Gotta Have It*, the man was relentless. It's easy to see Spike's salesmanship and single-mindedness as some extreme form of arrogance now that he's successful. But when he had no loot Spike was the same—he had a vision of himself and his work that he never wavered from. I never heard him express doubt, speculate about defeat, or worry about his ability to succeed. The walls were high but Spike always acted as if he knew where the door was. And when that door opened Spike moved through it quickly.

Two of the most exciting social events of my life involved *She's*. The first was a premiere party/sneaker jam at the Puck Building, which was the best throwdown it's been my pleasure to sweat at. Deejayed by Reggie Wells, the party was not simply a tribute to Spike but to the possibilities the film opened up. Long-suffering black filmmakers, New York–based actors, young musicians and writers, and artsy folks of various types were celebrating the opportunity to make their statement. "If Spike could do it, I can too" was the vibe though, as many of us later found out, monkey see is not always monkey do.

This same spirit of possibility was apparent outside the now defunct Cinema Studio at Sixty-sixth Street and Broadway where *She's* had a wonderful extended showing. I'll never forget exiting the number two train at Seventy-second Street and Broadway and walking down Broadway to the Cinema Studio the day the movie opened. Remember, I had cash in this thing, and despite the good reviews and hype it still hadn't made a dime. But it would. Outside the theater was a long, lively line of beautiful African-Americans. The peers of Nola, Greer, and the crew (but too many Mars) were all lined up to see themselves. Spike, in an early bout of the marketing mania we now know so well, was outside handing buttons to the throng. From opening day, long into its run, the ticket line at the Cinema Studio was the hippest club in New York. I used to go by just to see who was standing in line and catch the buzz. I may be leaning on this generational, coming-of-age theme a little hard, but I don't think so. The composition of those Cinema Studio crowds, the vibe at that Puck Building party, and the reception of the film all suggested that something special, something distinctive to us was occurring.

Robert Townsend's *Hollywood Shuffle* wasn't a cinematic work of art equal to Spike's debut, but it was just as crucial to the black film movement. His satire of Hollywood's abuse of African-American talent was pointed, funny, and surprisingly soft-hearted. Not only did the film give Townsend a platform (and capital), but it introduced the world to the formidable writing and acting skills of his partner, Keenen Ivory Wayans.

The BFF premiere for *Hollywood Shuffle* was held at a narrow little theater on Seventh Avenue. But the party after, held at the recently opened black bistro B. Smith's on Eighth Avenue, was wonderful. That night the bistro's elegant interior was overrun with black talent. I used my ticket stub as an autograph book and had it signed by Townsend, Warrington and Reggie Hudlin, Richard Wesley, actress Sheryl Lee Ralph, and several folks whose signatures I can no longer discern. It wasn't the throwdown of the *She's Gotta Have It* party. It was a warm, friendly family gathering that reflected Townsend's engaging personality. That Eddie Murphy was in the house, along with a large posse, was a sign of his support for Townsend, the BFF, and the energy surrounding black filmmakers. It did not go unnoticed.

While Townsend has gone on to have a prolific if commercially inconsistent career as a television and film director-producer, Spike has become an American icon whose every effort is greatly anticipated. I remember the day I realized how influential he'd become. In a front-page piece in *The New York Times*, not an article about Spike or film or black folks, there was a reference to Spike as if he were Pete Rose or Bugs Bunny or some other staple of pop culture. It was a passing reference, but since when did the old gray lady of journalism make casual allusions to black directors? Spike reached a level of celebrity that superseded his work. How did this happen?

Looking back, I can see that my often taciturn neighbor managed through his public statements, ambitions, and persona to seem part of several often warring constituencies without totally (for a time) alienating any of them. First, we must recall that the heart of the Reagan era saw an unprecedented move toward mainsteam visibility for blacks in media. While unemployment was rising to Depression levels in urban America (and crack dealing filled the vast economic and social chasm that joblessness created), white Americans were making Michael Jackson America's number-one pop star, with Whitney Houston, Lionel Richie, and Prince on his heels; they were choosing Oprah Winfrey over Phil Donahue as America's number-one talk show host; they were consistently pushing Eddie Murphy movies over the $70 million-plus mark; Magic Johnson and Michael Jordan were revolutionizing the playing and selling of NBA basketball; and the nation's number-one television series was *The Cosby Show*.

While some squeamish heterosexuals may have had a problem with Jackson's and Prince's androgyny, none of these people really challenged the status quo. Sure, they were strong-willed, often charismatic, idiosyncratic, but they were very affirming of the mainstream values of God, country, and hard work. I'd toss Jesse Jackson's first presidential campaign (pre-"Hymietown") into this mix as well. The reverend's embrace of electoral politics not only exhilarated minority voters and swelled the voter registration ranks, but sent a message that, despite racism, hard work and collective dedication could still work for African-Americans. And among the many messages communicated by Spike's emergence was that the nation's long-treasured Horatio Alger mythology was no joke. Spike's tale was as up-by-your-bootstraps as any Booker T. Washington could have advanced. He'd gone to Morehouse College, a haven for integrationist visionaries for decades (Martin Luther King is its most famous alumnus). Equally affirming of traditional-ist values was the prominence of his family in the film's making: sister Joie acted, brother David took stills used in the film and pub-licity, father Bill did the score. Within this context Spike's commer-cialization of his product through T-shirts, books, caps, and the character Mars Blackmon for Nike was the kind of merchandising cross-fertilization we'd come to expect from major media corpora-tions, efforts that in the eighties would define our reaction to a cul-tural production as much as the original product's quality (or lack of same).

For those who lived happily by an assimilationist credo or even neocon philosophy, the tale of Spike's making and selling of *She* was quite comforting. Over the years Spike's traditionalism would manifest itself in many ways—his dedication to jazz scores, his will-ful avoidance of drugs in *Do the Right Thing*, his contempt for blax-ploitation flicks, his embrace of television commercials. Yet Spike, from the start, also attached himself to the edgier, harder-to-assimi-late attitudes of eighties culture. His affectionate depiction of Mars Blackmon, one of film's first b-boys, is the most obvious example. So was his close association with those marketeers of militance, Public Enemy. He used their "Fight the Power" as the Greek chorus in *Do the Right Thing*, and his video of the track was a veritable cat-alogue of late-eighties in-your-face iconography (Tawana Brawley, Professor Griff, photos of Nelson Mandela).

Early in his career Spike, in interviews and on film, broke the rule that successful blacks don't air the race's dirty laundry in pub-lic. He regularly ripped Whoopi Goldberg's blue contacts, Steven Spielberg's *The Color Purple*, Rae Dawn Chong, Arsenio Hall, Eddie Murphy, and others whose work or behavior he found objection-able. The brother shot from the hip and, despite hostility from many blacks in Hollywood, he wouldn't shut up. The same critical fire burned throughout *School Daze*, an unflinching look at two of black America's most cherished institutions, the Greek societies and black universities, as well as that touchy topic, color consciousness. Spike's willingness to attack these symbols found favor with a grow-ing number of African-Americans who were weary of the positive-image mentality of so many established African-Americans. In theater, for example, George Wolfe's breakthrough play *The Colored Museum* was an intense depiction of racism and black self-delusion. Rap music was already, in the work of KRS-One and Public Enemy, starting to be similarly judgmental in 1987 and 1988.

Most central to Spike's early street credibility was something else he shared with KRS-One and P.E.—a fixation on Malcolm X. It's hard to remember now, but there was a time before the "X" hat, before Denzel Washington in Malcolm's spectacles, before the "X" potato chips, a time when embracing Malcolm X was a radical gesture. "By any means necessary" was still a phrase of confrontation and not a glib slogan in the mouths of marketers. Spike was a vocal champion of Malcolm X in the late eighties, which made him a kindred spirit with voices of the disenfranchised and fed up.

One other constituency that Spike appealed to may prove, in the long run, to be his strongest long-term supporters. Because of his training at NYU, his New York base, artistic ambition, and many stylistic flourishes (what I call Spikisms), Lee has emerged as a central obsession of the film cognoscenti. In an era of slick market-generated filmmaking, Spike and Oliver Stone are the only major American directors who consistently make cinematically and thematically challenging work. Political themes—sexual (*She's Gotta Have It*), intraracial (*School Daze*), interracial (*Do the Right Thing, Jungle Fever, X*)—fuel his most provocative features. Critics and op-ed page writers have ground out reams of negative and positive copy about them. Talk shows and college courses have been centered around his efforts. Even everyday conversation has been influenced by his films. For anyone deeply interested in our nation's film culture, he became the first African-American auteur to really matter. And as his complaints about the voting for the Palme d'Or in Cannes and campaigning for the Oscar for *X* suggest, he cares deeply about his acceptance in the places where cinematic reputations are solidified.

Many African-American filmmakers have made a mark since 1987, but no one has displaced him. In fact Spike has, for critics here and in Europe, risen above the black film dialogue and held his own in Hollywood at large. As long as Spike wants to make movies I see him finding funding, either from the U.S. studios or foreign investors (who, in this increasingly conglomerated world, are almost the same thing). There are few filmmakers of any color for whom I'd wish the same.

One last point: In several recent interviews Eddie Murphy has asserted that the wave of post–1987 African-American films is "a spinoff of my shit. . . . Young black people on-screen became marketable 'cause I was selling all those tickets." Well, that's simply not true. From his debut in *48 HRS.* in 1982 to 1986, the year of *She's Gotta Have It*, the only directing gigs for blacks in Hollywood came via rap films (*Beat Street, Krush Groove*) and music-driven projects (*The Last Dragon*). Prince was the only new black star to be supported by a studio (Warner Bros.). Murphy, like Pryor, was a movie star who generated revenue but did not create opportunities for filmmakers (directors, producers, screenwriters, etc.). If you look at films that were distributed and funded post-Eddie and post-Spike, it's clear where the spark for this wave (good or bad) was ignited. Although stars sell tickets, it is directors who create movements in cinema, and Spike, despite attempts to rewrite history, will always be the Jackie Robinson of this era.

FILM NERDS VERSUS COOL BIZZERS

From 1987 to 1990 the spark of *She's Gotta Have It* ignited little filmic brushfires all over the place. There was a real sense of possibility within the independent community that, inspired by Spike, crossed racial lines. I couldn't believe how many white young people I noticed in Greenwich Village and at the ultra-artsy Angelika Theater peering through copies of *Spike Lee's Gotta Have It*.

That book, which had been one of Spike's early dreams, instantly became a blueprint for independent filmmakers. In the world of African-American entertainment that I was toiling in at *Billboard*, the excitement level was palpable. "How can I get in this game?" That was the talk at record release parties. That was the conversation at screenings of indie films. The black music business and those in the black community interested in films had never had much contact. As I noted earlier, back in my *Amsterdam News* days, the Black Filmmaker Foundation world had been relatively isolated from more commercial parts of the culture. Spike and Townsend changed that. Now there was real synergy between young African-American filmmakers and music business folks. The filmmakers, mostly young men who'd attended prestigious schools like NYU, Harvard, Yale, and USC, still read comics, watched European classics on laser discs, wanted to direct music videos, and got up early as if they were practicing to be in production. A lot of them were what we'd call nerds.

The music bizzers, mostly young men who'd learned their game promoting parties, studied the charts, religiously dissected radio playlists, wanted to make movies with hit soundtracks, and never got to their offices before noon if they could help it. B-boys all the way.

Whatever the camp, they all shared one thing: They were ambitious in the extreme. At first the record people had the upper hand. The surge of hip-hop gave them a quick lift-up; it was easier to raise cash for a twelve-inch single than even a ten-minute short. The record industry had (and still has) more respect for black consumer dollars than the film industry. As time passed, however, the film nerds' stock rose and, in some cases, overshadowed the cool record bizzers. Today, in the mid-nineties, all types are trying to bust out of whatever aesthetic box they started in (Spike Lee, John Singleton, and the Hughes brothers all have record deals; Russell Simmons and Andre Harrell have television and film deals). But back then, when it was just starting to sink in that black commercial film was here to stay, the film nerds and the cool bizzers began feeling each other out.

As one of the links between the nerds and the b-boys, I caught the filmmaking bug myself in a big way. The proximity to all this energy was infectious. While still at *Billboard* and working on several book projects, I got involved with a series of film projects, of which only one turned out decently. All of them involved record business types who thought what Spike did was easy. After the relative success of *Krush Groove*, rap master Russell "Rush" Simmons was determined to control his own films. The ill-conceived and ill-fated *Tougher Than Leather* didn't scare him off. He paid me $4,000 to write a script for R & B singer Oran "Juice" Jones called *Cold Chillin' in a Hot Spot*. The title was the best thing about that project. I finished it and never looked back—gone!

My real mistake was to read and like a script written by the actor James Bond III. He'd been a child star, headlining the film *The Fish That Saved Pittsburgh* and doing a lot of theater. I'd met him briefly on the set of *School Daze*, in which he had a small part. Hajna Fishburne, Larry's now ex-wife, brought him over. His script was a black horror picture called *Temptation*. The premise was that the devil had possessed the soul of a beautiful woman and was using her as a tool for destroying weak-willed men. The lead character, a young minister facing a sudden crisis of faith, is the demon's ultimate target. Bond said he could make the film, start to finish, for $300,000.

Commercially it made sense. The black audience had always been a substantial part of the horror crowd. Artistically the most appealing thing about Bond's script was its use of black church rituals and imagery in the story. Catholicism had played a big role in *The Exorcist* and *The Omen*, and I figured African-American religiosity was ripe for confrontation with the devil. Record business entrepreneur Charles Huggins (the man behind Freddie Jackson) had been one of the many to curse himself for passing on investing in *She's*. He told me if anything came my way again to let him know. I set up a meeting between the two and, bingo, they got along instantly. For being the middleman, I asked for an executive producer credit and some points.

Bond and Huggins wrapped up a good cast, including Kadeem Hardison, Bill Nunn, Sam Jackson, Romy Clanton, Minnie Gentry, Melba Moore, and John Canada Terrell. Spike's photography director Ernest Dickerson agreed to shoot it. Larry Fishburne let us use his Bedford-Stuyvesant brownstone as the main production site, though the bulk of the film was shot in bars and uncompleted brownstones in Fort Greene just a few blocks from my house. *Temptation* actually might have been a fun, low-budget lark if Bond hadn't cast himself as the lead and directed. Most people don't have the perspective to direct themselves as Spike does. Bond, apparently feeling some kind of rivalry with Spike, was determined to prove he could do it. However, as anyone who's seen the film on cable or home video can testify, he couldn't. While Kadeem and Bill are actually pretty funny together, every time Bond comes on screen the film slows to a crawl. And his budget proved to be way off. Inexperience caught up to us when, still in the early stages of post-production, *Temptation* had already cost $350,000. When bills for items not even listed in the budget began showing up on Huggins's desk, he shut the film down for several months.

There was much bad blood on all sides. Calls went unreturned. Smiles turned to grimaces. Finally Troma, the schlock kingpins who gave the world *The Toxic Avenger*, bought the whole thing and put a little cash into some additional special effects. They "bicycled" the print into a few cities (they took one print and shipped it town to town instead of opening in multiple cities) and then made a killing in home video. I made virtually no money from the film, though I got my first screen credit on the horror epic *Def by Temptation* (Troma added the "Def" for "marketing" purposes).

I anticipated that my first producing experience was going to be fun. It was painful, frustrating, and embarrassing in the extreme. My lack of knowledge of filmmaking, my failure to understand the abilities of folks I was aiding, and my inability to have any creative input, all made for a truly horrible lesson. *Def by Temptation* knocked any cockiness I had for being down with Spike right out of my head. It was an ass-whipping I deserved. And there were plenty more coming.

Part Three

LOW-BUDGET
DEALS
1987–1990

1987

Robert Townsend's *Hollywood Shuffle*, put together with credit cards and short ends from other features, is an amusing, well-observed look at the conflicts of being a black actor in Hollywood. Co-written by Keenen Ivory Wayans, this film introduced a lot of great comic talent and made it clear that the new commercial black film movement was not a one-shot deal.

Actor Robert Townsend's *Hollywood Shuffle* helped the new wave in black film keep going. (Courtesy of Tinsel Townsend Productions.)

Denzel Washington is nominated for the best supporting actor Oscar for his performance as Steve Biko in the otherwise disappointing antiapartheid film *Cry Freedom*.

Morgan Freeman is nominated as best supporting actor for his work in *Street Smart*, in which he plays the most complex black pimp in film history. Pauline Kael opened her review of the film, "Is Morgan Freeman the greatest American actor?"

Disorderlies is a low point in Michael Schultz's career and hip-hop's cinematic history. In this film, the Fat Boys proved they were not the Three Stooges.

Eddie Murphy's concert film *Eddie Murphy Raw* fixates on the role of women in his life. Both mean and funny, Murphy's cynical view of the opposite sex confirms the suspicions of many hip-hop—age males. The film was directed by Robert Townsend and opens with a skit written by Keenen Ivory Wayans and Murphy.

Bill Cosby, whose "The Cosby Show" dominates prime-time television, stars in the year's most celebrated flop, *Leonard Part 6*. The gap between TV and film audiences was made clear by this picture's commercial failure.

Ousmane Sembène's *Camp de Thiaroye* (written and co-directed by Thierno Faty Sow) is the first pan-African feature produced completely without European technical aid or co-financing. All the money for this historic epic came from Algeria, Tunisia, and Senegal. At Camp de Thiaroye in 1944, Senegalese infantrymen returning from the war are interred instead of being allowed to return to their home villages. Tension between the Senegalese and French soldiers mounts and results in a bloody insurrection on November 30, 1944.

Danny Glover, after years of quality work, reaches national stardom as Mel Gibson's detective partner in *Lethal Weapon*.

1988

Spike Lee's *School Daze* attempts to mix a social critique of African-American color consciousness, a celebration of black college life, anti-apartheid message, and big musical production numbers. It's not a sweet blend, but it has many fine ingredients. Larry Fishburne has his first lead role, though Giancarlo Esposito, Bill Nunn, Jasmine Guy, and Spike himself, with better-defined characters, come off stronger. The film contains go-go music's one certifiable radio hit, "Da Butt," and helped spark a wave of interest in black colleges. The production team that would be the backbone of Spike's work (director of photography Ernest Dickerson, production designer Wynn Thomas, casting director Robi Reed, costume director Ruthe Carter) came together on *School Daze*.

Eddie Murphy shocks the film business and millions of viewers by criticizing the poor representation of blacks in the film industry during the Academy Awards.

Giancarlo Esposito berates Spike Lee in Lee's first studio feature, *School Daze*. (Courtesy of Columbia Pictures.)

- The invaluable *Blacks in American Films and Television: An Illustrated Encyclopedia* (Simon & Schuster) is published by historian Donald Bogle.

- With *Little Nikita* and *Shoot to Kill,* Sidney Poitier returns to the big screen. In both these features he plays police authority figures in pieces that don't challenge him. The real Poitier comeback vehicle is *Simple Justice,* a TV movie about attorney (later Supreme Court justice) Thurgood Marshall two years later. Poitier's majestic presence is well suited to the part of that landmark barrister.

- *Colors,* Dennis Hopper's policer about two white cops, still manages to showcase the L.A. gang culture in a feature for the first time. Damon Wayans is hilarious as a crazed gang member. Ice-T provides the chilling title rap.

- Run-D.M.C.'s *Tougher Than Leather,* directed by record producer Rick Rubin, is inept even by blaxploitation standards. Most of the money for the film is put up by Rubin, the group's manager, Russell Simmons, and the three group members. It makes less than $5 million. Significantly it is New Line Cinema's first attempt to reach the black youth market and the last film explicitly and solely about rap without context. From here on, rappers and rap music would become defining elements in black inner-city dramas.

Only 120 of 6,500 members of the Writers Guild or 2 percent are black. The Directors Guild list 195 blacks out of 8,558 or 2.25 percent. Meanwhile 4,033 of the Screen Actors Guild are black or 5.7 percent.

Moving is another DOA Richard Pryor vehicle. His stardom and his health are both on the wane.

Eddie Murphy gives his most endearing performance as an African prince seeking his wife in America in *Coming to America*. Under the direction of John Landis (*Trading Places*), Arsenio Hall and John Amos are also outstanding. The film employs more blacks on screen than all Murphy's previous films combined. Despite its success the film will probably be remembered more for Art Buchwald's plagiarism suit than the quality of the film itself.

Keenen Ivory Wayans establishes his comic voice with his direction and writing of *I'm Gonna Git You Sucka*, a blaxploitation parody with raw humor and big sight gags. Memorable comic turns are taken by Damon Wayans, Chris Rock, Anne-Marie Johnson, Jim Brown, Isaac Hayes, Dawn Lewis, and Antonio Fargas. The film makes $13 million.

Jazz buff Clint Eastwood directs *Bird*, a long, moody, and unsatisfying biography of saxophonist Charlie Parker. Forest Whitaker is excellent as the self-destructive genius. But the film is more about Parker's relationship with his white wife than the musical innovations that made him worth immortalizing.

1989

The controversial *Do the Right Thing* elevates Spike Lee to the top rank of world filmmaking. Several critics, black and white, predict Lee's look at a day in the life of a tense Bedford-Stuyvesant block will generate violence. Instead it generates piles of press, most of it positive. It ends up on many year-end ten-best lists and earns Lee an Academy Award nomination for best screenplay. The use of Public Enemy's "Fight the Power" as a Greek chorus throughout the film is the best cinematic use of rap music to date. Danny Aiello gains a best supporting actor nomination for his work as Sal, the pizza shop owner, while Rosie Perez, John Turturro, and the exciting comic Robin Harris also shine. Ernest Dickerson's cinematography and Wynn Thomas's creation of a vital Brooklyn block are innovative. The film makes $27 million.

Spurred on by the examples of his peers, Eddie Murphy directs *Harlem Nights*, a failed attempt at a *Sting*-styled period film with a great cast (Richard Pryor, Redd Foxx, Della Reese) that simply wasn't as funny as it could have been.

See No Evil, Hear No Evil is a fitful end to the Richard Pryor—Gene Wilder collaboration. Pryor looks sick.

Robert Townsend displays some humor (and a bad accent) and Denzel Washington his tanned good looks in the totally forgettable Caribbean caper movie *The Mighty Quinn*.

Euzhan Palcy's *A Dry White Season*, based on André Brink's anti-apartheid novel, is the first big-budget film about South Africa made by a black filmmaker. Palcy does her best to make her film serve the black characters in ways *Cry Freedom* and *A World Apart* did not, but too much of the story centers around the political education of a naive white man. Marlon Brando makes a showy appearance as a judge, while the South African native Zakes Mokae serves as the film's moral center.

Morgan Freeman receives an Oscar nomination for best actor for his role as a gentle Southern chauffeur in *Driving Miss Daisy*. Whites loved this film, but to blacks it was old snake oil in a new bottle.

Charles Lane, a longtime black indie filmmaker, makes his commercial debut with the Island-distributed *Sidewalk Stories*. This gentle film is both silent and black and white, yet heartwrenching in its depiction of a homeless painter taking care of a lost little girl. Though poorly marketed, *Sidewalk Stories* confirms Lane's talent and gets him the first solid Hollywood offers of his long career.

1990

The Sundance Film Festival, held in January, is a coming-of-age for black cinema. Black critic Armond White is a festival judge and plays a key advocacy role for Wendell Harris's *Chameleon Street*, which wins the critics' award. Charles Burnett's *To Sleep with Anger* receives critical kudos as well. *House Party*, directed by Reggie Hudlin and produced by Warrington Hudlin, wins the filmmaker's award (voted on by the directors in attendance) and the award for best cinematography.

Charles Burnett makes his commercial theatrical debut with *To Sleep with Anger*. Danny Glover, who executive produced, plays a trickster figure who almost destroys a black Los Angeles family. The ghosts of Africa by way of the Deep South inform this parable of old evil infecting a contemporary scene. This film may be the most accomplished work of the current black film wave.

After winning the top award at the Sundance Film Festival, *Chameleon Street* can't find major distribution. Wendell Harris's idiosyncratic film, based on the real-life escapades of two disturbed hustlers, Erik Dupin and William Douglas Street, is another up-by-the-bootstraps black film saga. Harris, who shot the film in Detroit, stars as the man whose identity is in constant flux. One of the few films ever made about a black white-collar criminal.

Reggie Hudlin's *House Party* is a delightful, free-spirited teen comedy anchored by Robin Harris, the most beloved African-American comic of this period. Hudlin's genial direction and the script's good humor make it a genuine heir to *Cooley High*'s mantle. It is one of the few films to explore the party-hardy side of hip-hop culture. Martin Lawrence provided sharp comic relief for the rappers-turned-actors Kid 'N' Play. The film makes $28 million.

Spike Lee's *Mo' Better Blues* is a triumph of set design, styling, and production values but as drama it falls flat. Wesley Snipes emerges as a sex symbol in a dazzling supporting role.

Reggie Hudlin (right), director of *House Party* and *Boomerang,* with the author. (Courtesy of Kim Weston.)

- Sidney Poitier's *Ghost Dad* with Bill Cosby feels like an extended sitcom pilot.

- *Paris Is Burning*, a documentary by white indie filmmaker Jennie Livingston, is an immediate cult classic. This look at the flamboyant world of New York's black and Latino drag queens gives voice to a segment of the African-American community totally ignored by the black mainstream. The dedication, style, and humor of the divas is undeniably entertaining.

- With *The White Girl,* longtime television broadcaster Tony Brown puts $1 million where his mouth is. He funds, directs, and then takes his film on a Oscar Micheaux—like journey to cities across America. Alas, this story of a young woman who becomes addicted to cocaine ("the white girl") is too preachy to be affecting as drama or cautionary tale. A very noble failure.

ONE PARTY = THREE PICTURES

I once saw a photo of a party held on Fourth Avenue in Brooklyn in 1987. It was a housewarming for the offices of a new record and artist management company called Uptown, headed by a smart, eager ex-rapper named Andre Harrell. Everyone was feeling Brooklyn vapors at this time, so Andre decided his new MCA-financed company would be based near, but not in, Fort Greene. The party was a happening affair, as Uptown parties continue to be to this day. The picture I refer to depicts Andre, Russell Simmons, Warrington and Reggie Hudlin, and a few others in a highly cele-bratory mood on the top floor of the Uptown duplex. Like many parties I remember from that period it had more import than just being a good way to sweat and get phone numbers.

At least three films that are part of the post–*She's Gotta Have It* wave of African-American-themed films were affected by relation-ships represented by that picture at the Uptown party. This tangled saga started a few days earlier, when I introduced the Hudlins to Andre and Russell. Reggie and Warrington, like many other black indie filmmakers, had been trying to crack the black music video scene. Because I worked at *Billboard* and had ties to the BFF, I could act as a middleman.

Andre and the Hudlins immediately hit it off. Russell liked them as well, though he never became as tight with them as Andre did. Both these rap moguls had seen Reggie's student-film version of *House Party* and *Kold Waves* from his Harvard days and soon started showing up at BFF functions. And, of course, they weren't alone. In the two years following *She's Gotta Have It*, everyone was looking for the next Spike.

Russell and Run-D.M.C. were preparing to do a film, *Tougher Than Leather*, to be released in conjunction with their follow-up to their breakthrough album *Raising Hell*. They were looking for a director and, hot as Run-D.M.C. was at that moment, everyone knew it would be a plum job. Reggie campaigned heavily for the gig but Rick Rubin, who co-owned Def Jam records with Rush, was writing the script and was determined to direct. (According to

Spike's book *Do the Right Thing*, Russell did offer him the directing job.) Russell had to tell Reggie no out of loyalty to his partner. *Tougher Than Leather* under Rubin's direction went on to make less than $5 million for New Line Cinema and, with a lengthy delay in releasing the accompanying soundtrack, damaged the trio's career. Andre did hire the Hudlins to direct the first two Uptown videos. Warrington directed "Uptown Kickin' It," a compilation cut that introduced all Andre's acts. I even did a cameo as a record executive and Andre played himself. Heavy D & the Boyz would turn out to be the only one among the original group to become a significant rap star, but the highlight of "Uptown Kickin' It" was the three-man group Groove B Chill, who danced and sang/rapped the song's climax. Reggie handled directing chores on Heavy D's "Mr. Big Stuff," Uptown's first hit. But again, even as background people, Groove B Chill were lively and funny. The Hudlins were so excited by the multimedia potential of the trio that at one point they investigated managing them.

Meanwhile, Reggie was making progress in Hollywood. He drafted a script for the Time–Janet Jackson movie at the request of A & M Films. A studio had purchased the option on *Kold Waves* based on Reggie's student-film version. And, ultimately most important, the Hudlins were talking with New Line about making *House Party* a full-length feature movie. For a long time Groove B Chill were the Hudlins' choice for the parts eventually played by Kid 'N' Play and Martin Lawrence.

A key reason that casting didn't happen was an aborted video for GUY produced and directed by the Hudlins. GUY, the original new jack swing band, was on Uptown and Andre had hired the Hudlins to supply the visuals for "Groove Me." A very stylized video, directed by Reggie, was shot at the Apollo Theater. But Gene Griffin, the band's manager and Andre's antagonist over control of GUY, didn't like it. As a result the Hudlins' video was scrapped and, upset with Andre for caving in to Griffin, Warrington and Reggie decided to look elsewhere for *House Party* leads. Groove B Chill did end up in *House Party*, but in small supporting roles.

The very germ of the third film I mentioned actually took hold in a way at that same, infamous party. A young novelist named Trey

Ellis had shown up with Reggie. Ellis is a sophisticated, well-spoken guy. However, to several members of the Uptown crew, he reeked of corny. In the condescending way the self-consciously hip have, Uptowners found Ellis's demeanor amusing. At that same party was a young woman who was notorious in our circle for dancing suggestively with two and three men at a time. I don't know if she and Ellis even exchanged words that night, but Andre was struck by the idea of how such an incongruous match could be made.

One evening a few weeks later we began sketching out a story in my Fort Greene living room about a stuck-up black man and a black fly girl falling in love. While Ellis's studied mannerisms inspired the character Waymon Tinsdale, the woman who'd eventually be named Natalie in the script was a composite of any number of vivacious young women we saw nightly at clubs like Nell's and MK's.

Andre had, at one point, discussed this project with the Hudlins. But after the GUY video conflict, the Hudlins concentrated on their own films, while Andre picked black-owned Atlantis Productions to make *Go Natalie!* happen. Atlantis producer-writer Pam Gibson and director Rolando Hutson were two of the first blacks to make a dent in the music video field. Russell gave them their first jobs and Andre would be supportive as well. Atlantis got the "Groove Me" job and did a more party-oriented video that pleased all involved. There were plenty of "Go!" girls in the video and Andre felt they'd be perfect for the project.

There's an interesting subtext to this saga. There was at the time a lot of hostility between the folks from indie film and those making music videos. The indie folks, often with film school training, looked down at their less-pedigreed competitors as hacks. The videomakers, many of whom came either out of commercials or the music biz, thought the indie folks were snotty and uncommercial.

This all added a little spice to Andre's commitment to Atlantis. At first Andre was going to finance the film himself. But better judgment, probably in the form of accountants and agents, made him think seek out OPM ("other people's money"). From roughly 1988, when Andre first announced the Uptown-Atlantis hookup, to principal photography in the spring of 1991, the film was on and off again several times. The force that kept the dream alive was Pam

Gibson. When I stepped off to work on a book or Andre focused on building Uptown, Pam was the constant who worked diligently on the script and budget. Sometime in 1990, Island World Films, owned by Chris Blackwell and the distributor of *She's*, became involved with the project. This opportunity, instead of making everything run more smoothly, in fact exacerbated some ongoing conflicts. There were financial concerns over being reimbursed for monies spent on the project during the pre-Island years. There were disputes over production credits on the film. The folks at Island were never in love with Hutson's work and only Andre's insistence kept him aboard. All these fights, and a couple of others, raged right up through the first week of shooting, when Hutson was fired four days into production.

Given my creative role, this experience was a lot more painful than *Def by Temptation*, for which I had been really just a facilitator. Rarely had I felt so helpless in my work. Decisions were made that affected me but on which I had no input. People said one thing to me and another to my partners. There were moments when I felt I couldn't trust anybody, even people I'd known for years. As one of the Island guys cheerily told my attorney, "Everybody gets raped on their first picture, so just tell Nelson to bend over."

But don't get me wrong. I got a lot out of the *Go Natalie!* (eventually *Strictly Business*) experience. Pam and I spent much of the summer of 1990 in West Hollywood hotel suites earning $700 a week per diem and turning in pages—just like real screenwriters. When not spending afternoons working on dialogue and story, we visited Disneyland with Pam's daughter, Danielle, wandered around West Hollywood, and became acquainted with the Beverly Center. I got into my first jacuzzi, went on a pilgrimage to America's new favorite ghetto, Compton, and got caught up in a typically transitory L.A. love affair with a woman I met at the trendy Roxbury's restaurant-disco.

Being a nondriver I was geographically restricted. And I soon learned that young black men didn't usually wander on foot around West Hollywood. I got evil stares from white folks in L.A. that I'd never felt in a lifetime of New York living. That summer I first saw that *Colors* was not a white fantasy and N.W.A. not a black nightmare, but that there was a tension between black and white, have and have-nots, in the City of Angels, the depth of which we didn't yet understand back East.

When I finally went back to New York Pam stayed on, continuing to work with Island. I had little else to do with the film, though I was on the set the day they fired Hutson, saw dailies on a regular basis, and threw in a line or two when I was around. Kevin Hooks, former child actor and veteran TV director, came in under duress and did a good job under the circumstances. He seemed frustrated by many of the casting and location decisions made before he came on board, yet he held the film together like a champ.

The final product looked like a tight Disney formula comedy of the eighties. Things seemed to happen because the story dictated they happen and not for organic reasons. The film was made by black producers, writers, and directors, yet the vision of the white Hollywood financiers weighed heavily on it. One of the script's reasons for existing was its special black dynamic; I think that's precisely why Island stuck with the project for so long. During production I remember Warner Bros. development executive Billy Gerber telling me that the studio picked the film up because they loved the script. But in the end the film was merely wholesome, and lacked the New York flavor we'd envisioned those many years ago.

Strictly Business tested incredibly well. I was told it received *Batman*-like approval ratings. At a test screening I attended at a mall outside L.A., folks cheered the coming together of the buppie and the b-boy that was the film's climax. Oh, I should mention that Halle Berry tested very high with males. But Warner Bros.' salesmanship was wack. From the one-sheet to the trailer to the logo to the test-marketed generic title, *Strictly Business* gave off a low-rent, home video vibe.

The premiere was a great night in New York. My mother and nieces sat with me at the Ziegfeld and cheered when my name came on screen at the beginning, then joined in the big ovation when it was over. There were handshakes and congratulations all around. The Uptown-designed party rocked until way after three in the morning.

Then on opening night, November 8, reality kicked in. In Andre's limo, packed with actors and friends, we hit several theaters that were, at best, half full. I'll never forget the sound of the dialogue echoing through a vast expanse of empty seats at one of the big rooms at a Thirty-fourth Street multiplex. If that's what they mean by the sound of one hand clapping, it's a pretty depressing noise. The last thing I remember about that Friday was lying on the floor of the limo gurgling champagne out of the bottle. They say failure is good for the soul. Well, we were all cleansed that night.

Part Four

B-BOYS, BUPPIES & THE ODD BOHO 1991

The breakthrough of *She's Gotta Have It* and Spike's growing visibility; the work of Robert Townsend, Keenen Ivory Wayans, and Reggie Hudlin; the tenacity of a number of Hollywood vets and indie auteurs who'd been knocking on the door for years; financing institutions of various kinds finally opening their eyes to the potential of black films by black people: all these elements combined in 1991 to get made and theatrically distributed more features directed by African-Americans than in any previous year in American cinema history. Nineteen were originally scheduled. Some, like *Juice*, weren't released until 1992. A few were announced and never showed up.

During that year, if I could find one of those films playing somewhere I made it my business to see it. The ones I liked I saw several times. Even a few I didn't like I often saw again to figure out what I could learn from their failures. Interwoven around my views of the films are anecdotes that, I hope, fill in some of the backstory on the conditions under which black films get made in Hollywood.

I've listed the films here chronologically, according to their official release date.

New Jack City (Warner Bros.)

Throughout the eighties Warner Bros. studio was the home of high-octane, bloody action flicks with *Lethal Weapon* and ex-bodyguard Steven Seagal's flicks prime examples. Black audiences were a substantial part of the action-film audience, so it was appropriate that Bugs Bunny's studio bankrolled the first successful balls-to-the-wall, black action movie since the blaxploitation era.

Warner Bros. had, through black producers George Jackson and Doug McHenry, been involved with hip-hop moviemaking since the mid-eighties (*Krush Groove*, *Disorderlies*). *New Jack City* was originally about the life and legend of Harlem heroin kingpin Nicky "Mr. Untouchable" Barnes, a real-life black Godfather whom the feds nailed in the seventies at the urging of President Carter. Innovative journalist Barry Michael Cooper, who'd written a number of brilliant crime stories for *The Village Voice* (and who'd coined the musical phrase "new jack swing" for the latest movement in black pop), came on board to give the script contemporary flavor. Since crack became a mass-market item in the mid-eighties, teenaged drug dealers were turning into instant millionaires and the level of violence in urban America had soared. Barry brought his intimate knowledge of this world to bear on the script.

There was a lot of debate over who'd direct *New Jack City* and Mario Van Peebles, son of Melvin, actor in many low-budget flicks and active television director, landed the gig. Some say Van Peebles fan Clint Eastwood lobbied the studio for his friend (they'd worked together on *Heartbreak Ridge*). The combination of Van Peebles, Cooper, and the producers was volatile. All had very strong visions of the material, visions that often conflicted. Yet out of this creative conflict came a sexy, quickly paced, totally entertaining movie. Essential to its appeal was a *Young Guns* cast of hip black male actors. Crooner Christopher Williams had quickly emerged as a sex symbol with the release of his first album. Comic Chris Rock had been well regarded since he debuted nationally as Eddie Murphy's protégé on an HBO special. Ice-T was one of the originators of Los Angeles's gangster rap.

However, *New Jack City*'s key players were two relatively unknown New York actors, Wesley Snipes as Nino Brown and Allen Payne as his sidekick Gee Money. Snipes had been bubbling under for a while with roles in *Wildcats* and *Major League*, and a striking performance in Michael Jackson's "Bad" video. Payne had modeled, acted on the New York stage, and done some television. Snipes was charming, threatening, and sexy—the first black macho-action-flick leading man since the reigns of Jim Brown and Richard Roundtree. Supporting Snipes, Payne gave an underappreciated but solid performance. They played off each other smoothly and, lightly, tapped into homoerotic undertones in the characters' relationship. They called each other "brother." Yet when Payne knelt before Snipes to beg for his life, there was another, more intimate relationship suggested between the two.

Perhaps influenced by *Do the Right Thing*, Van Peebles and director of photography Francis Kenny used dutch angles and a colorful palette that enhanced the energetic story.

Just as aggressive as the film was the *New Jack City* soundtrack.

Packed with new jack swing and hard-edged rap (Ice T's "New Jack Hustler" is one of his best singles), the record was a snappy souvenir of the film that would dominate black radio for most of 1991. On all levels *New Jack City* was a shrewdly designed, produced, directed, and marketed piece of commercial filmmaking not atypical of the studio that gave us *Batman* and the *Lethal Weapon* series.

Which is why the film's opening weekend violence was so disturbing. There was a riot in front of the theater playing *New Jack City* in Westwood, California. There were fatal shootings near theaters in Detroit and Brooklyn. Each incident was different. For example, the Westwood riot was blamed on overselling of tickets and poor crowd control by theater management. No patron looked at Snipes killing someone on-screen and then decided to do likewise. What happened on the opening night of *New Jack City*, much like the night that a major rap tour hits a town, is that the event becomes the place to be for all elements of black youth. The same attitudes and conflicts that exist outside the theater are brought inside. In many cases these shootings would have happened somewhere else—it just happened that the film's appeal too often placed enemies in violent proximity.

Warner Bros. sold *New Jack City* with the same gusto as for its other action films. However, with the level of black-on-black violence now higher than ever before, black filmmakers, as creators of black youth events, have to factor that reality into their art and salesmanship. *New Jack City* served notice that films dealing with ghettocentric subject matter would have to be marketed sensitively or run the risk of aggravating the conditions they purport to explore.

The Five Heartbeats (Fox)

It is opening night for *New Jack City* and the murmuring of a packed house fills the cavernous Mann Chinese Theatre's main room. The crowd is young, hyped, and ready for a good time. It is the crowd that made *House Party* a hit, the crowd that supports Steven Seagal, the crowd that's been down with Eddie Murphy for years. It is the crowd that turned out opening night for all the black film hits of '91.

When the trailer for *The Five Heartbeats* appears on screen, there is an initial surge of energy. But as the trailer continues on, with images of Robert Townsend, Michael Wright, and the other actors flashing on screen and a pseudo–R & B oldie playing on the soundtrack, the audience stays silent. When the trailer ends with Townsend at the piano and a final burst of R & B, the *New Jack City* crowd doesn't clap, cheer, or even mumble. There is, in fact, no discernible reaction.

In New York a few weeks later at the Black Filmmaker Foundation premiere, *The Five Heartbeats* plays like a dream. People cheer. They clap often. The crowd is like that at most BFF premieres—adult professionals for whom the saga of a 1960s vocal group is not abstract history but personal nostalgia. At the party after people talk about how "We need more films like this!" while criticizing *New Jack City* for its "negative images."

Ultimately the audience that launched *New Jack City* didn't bother with *The Five Heartbeats* and not enough of those for whom *The Five Heartbeats* truly resonated paid to see it. The fate of Townsend's heartwarming film was that simple and sad. The differences between *New Jack City* and *The Five Heartbeats* were defined by hip-hop aggression versus R & B conviction, by a moviegoing youth audience versus homebody adults. The contrast between these films and their very different commercial fates revealed one of the central conflicts in black film and the overall community.

The Five Heartbeats (like *Mo' Better Blues* the year before) attempted both to tell a story and to capture the essence of a non–hip-hop style of African-American music. But the *New Jack* film audience either was not interested in or was ignorant of their connection to rhythm and blues and bebop. The reasons for this intracultural blind spot are legion: bad schools, black radio's unwillingness to program the spectrum of African-American music, a profound communications breakdown between black generations, and the overall disinterest of Americans in history.

The result is that period black films, be they *The Five Heartbeats*, *A Rage in Harlem*, *Glory*, or any that use something besides hip-hop music as their aesthetic spine, do not appeal to the young, active, black moviegoing crowd. A substantial audience for all these films does exist on network TV, on cable, and in home video. But it's clear anything with a substantial black theme that's period (*Driving Miss Daisy*, *The Color Purple*) needs the strong support of black women (and white ones) to thrive theatrically.

A Rage in Harlem (Miramax)

Friday night, May 10, 1991. Hollywood Boulevard. Hamburger Hamlet. I'm having a strawberry milkshake and a burger. My date is munching on french fries. We're killing time until the 10:15 showing of *A Rage in Harlem* at the Mann. I'd seen Bill Duke's film at a New York screening but I was curious how it would play on the left coast.

Like the Chester Himes detective novels, the tone shifted a little too glibly between farce and brutality, but stars Danny Glover, Gregory Hines, and Forest Whitaker were fine, as was Badja Djola as a backwoods villain. However, the true star of *A Rage in Harlem* was Robin Givens as the femme fatale Immabelle. Overcoming the bad publicity generated by her controversial marriage to heavyweight champ Mike Tyson, she gave an incredibly sexy, profoundly troubled, and fascinating performance.

Sitting in Hamburger Hamlet that Friday night, the last person I expected to see was a celebrity. When a music biz friend from New York walked in, I waved him over. We were kicking it when he turned and yelled, "Robin!" In jeans, jacket, and a baseball cap squeezed down low on her forehead, Robin Givens strolled over to the table. Turns out they were going to the 10:15 show too!

We sat in the back row of the theater with Givens curled up in an aisle seat watching herself on screen. There are few experiences more bizarre than watching actors watch themselves. The Givens of *Rage* was self-confident, Southern, sultry. The Givens sitting two seats away looked as anxious as a deer in a hunter's gunsights, her real voice a strange echo of Katharine Hepburn's New England lockjaw. Whenever male audience members howled at her on-screen saunter or at something she said, Givens seemed to shrink in her seat, as if she wished she could disappear right into the cushion. Still, if they'd given out black film Oscars at the end of 1991, Givens would have won, hands down, for best female lead performance of the year.

Straight Out of Brooklyn (Samuel Goldwyn)

"So, what didya think?" I asked four different people who'd seen Matty Rich's first effort. With the kindness of cousins they all basically replied, "He's only nineteen." They meant it as a compliment, but I took it as an excuse.

As much as I admired Matty Rich's bootstraps saga of raising money via a black radio talk show, I wasn't very impressed by *Straight Out of Brooklyn*. That it was gritty didn't make it art. The really artful thing about *Straight Out of Brooklyn* wasn't the film at all but the public relations work of Terrie Williams.

Working with the Reverend Jesse Jackson, Eddie Murphy, *Essence* magazine, and many of America's most important figures, Williams emerged in the mid-eighties as the nation's most prominent black publicist. But her campaign for Matty had to be her greatest achievement. She took a modest film, its young filmmaker, and a rags-to-riches story, and got him as much press in 1991 as Spike Lee and John Singleton. By the end of the year *Straight Out of Brooklyn* had made only $2.7 million playing mostly at art houses, but Matty, in his Lee-like glasses and graffiti-splattered overalls, was a household word in black America.

Jungle Fever (Universal)

Spike's fifth film had *major* hype. As America's most controversial filmmaker (perhaps right after Oliver Stone), Spike again tackled a contentious subject—interracial romance. The poster shows a white female hand and a black male hand locked together. Wesley Snipes and Annabella Sciorra, who played the taboo lovers, made the cover of *Newsweek*. Hot stuff, all this. The funny thing was that this interracial sex thing wasn't really what the film was about.

The relationship between black architect Flipper Purify and his secretary Angie remained highly unmotivated and quite murky. Although no one could have anticipated it, Flipper Purify would be one of 1991's great missed opportunities. *Jungle Fever* was released in early summer. Later in the year two historic events, the Clarence Thomas Supreme Court confirmation hearings and basketball star Earvin "Magic" Johnson's announcement that he had contracted the HIV virus through heterosexual intercourse, would make black sexuality front-page news. But it wasn't just sex that became the subject of debate, it was power relationships in sex. Just as Anita Hill claimed Thomas abused his power over her to harass her and Johnson's star status made women submit to his lust, Purify had a similar edge over his secretary Angie. Although it wasn't verbalized in the script's emphasis on race, the class dynamic between Purify and Angie perhaps had as much to do with their sexual relationship as his drafting board. By pulling Purify and Angie from such obviously different socioeconomic backgrounds (despite the advantages of whiteness, Angie was clearly economically inferior to her black lover), Spike invites this reading of the film. Yet he doesn't wrestle with it enough, at least for me, which accounts for the flatness of some of their scenes.

In contrast, the depiction of the dysfunctional families that surrounded the two protagonists was really sharp and insightful. I remember being both moved and impressed by that aspect of the film as I exited the premiere at Times Square's National Theater. Purify's brood is a study in extremes. He's an ambitious buppie with a beautiful mulatto wife (Lonette McKee) and an adorable daughter. His father (Ossie Davis) is a fierce Christian, his mother (Ruby Dee) subservient to his father, and their other son, Gator (the magnificent Sam Jackson) is a charming, manipulative crackhead whose drug habit leads his family inexorably toward tragedy.

Angie's family is haunted by the death of her mother. Her father is a racist and her brothers narrow-minded and lazy. All three are old-school chauvinists who rely on Angie to cook, clean, and otherwise accommodate them, while ignoring the sacrifices she makes for them. As a result she yearns for freedom, a freedom that her affair with Purify symbolizes.

Her brothers are sometime members of an ad hoc group of Italian men who congregate daily at a Bensonhurst luncheonette.

Sitting at the tables and counter of Paulie Carbone's (John Turturro) establishment are men of various ages who spend much of the time reinforcing each other's prejudices. Often the odd man out is Paulie, a sensitive, dreamy romantic who once dated Angie, but now has a strong crush on Orin Goode (Tyra Ferrell), a member of one of Bensonhurst's few black families. Aside from suffering from a mild case of jungle fever, Paulie's biggest problem is his father (Anthony Quinn), another dominating patriarch lost without a wife to dominate. But while Angie's father is the embodiment of working-class prejudice, Quinn brings an overwrought, operatic note to the role.

Many of the scenes involving these tense families are insightful, funny, and powerful. As false as some of the dialogue between Angie and Flipper sometimes sounds, it's offset by the witty banter at the luncheonette, Gator's escalating manipulation of his mother, and the searing final confrontation between Gator and his Bible-thumping father.

The father executes his wayward offspring in the name of the Lord as Mahalia Jackson plays on the soundtrack in one of the most stunning sequences in Spike's career. In that one scene the destruction that drugs have visited upon African-Americans, the rigid morality of born-again Christianity, and the devastating generation gap that shaped blacks in the eighties are all smartly captured by Spike, director of photography Ernest Dickerson, and editor Sam Pollard.

Spike had been criticized for ignoring drugs in his earlier urban drama, *Do the Right Thing*. In *Jungle Fever* drugs, along with the family, form the film's thematic backbone. Typically Spike's vision of drug addiction is more impressionistic than literal. Using Stevie Wonder's "Livin' for the City" as background score, Spike takes Purify into a surreal crackhouse in search of Gator. With its smoky interior, crack pipes flashing like beacons, and doomed inhabitants, the place is a 1990s inferno. Some folks argued that this wasn't a real crackhouse, but it was completely in keeping with Spike's often hyperbolic vision of everyday reality.

Sam Jackson, who won a special award at Cannes for his performance, actually dominates the film in his supporting role. Like Freddie in *Superfly* and Chris Rock in *New Jack City*, the role of the drug victim is one that touches deep chords of empathy in blacks. Jackson gives a nuanced depiction of how addiction can destroy an addict and weaken a family. The addict can become the dominant presence in a family since, over time, his or her illness can sap all the family's reserves of good will, love, and money. While Snipes's buppie is our nominal protagonist, it is Gator's actions that ignite *Jungle Fever*'s most memorable moments.

Boyz N the Hood (Columbia)

During the spring of 1990 Russell Simmons was raving about a script titled *Boyz N the Hood*. Rush had been negotiating with Jon Peters and Columbia regarding a movie deal and somewhere along the line Columbia slipped him a script by a black USC graduate named John Singleton. Rush isn't a big reader so when he raved about a piece of writing I paid attention.

Reading it *was* exhilarating. Here was great narrative storytelling that captured the trials and choices young black men are confronted with. In its three central boys—the gang banger, the football player, the aspiring college boy—young Singleton had managed to deftly cover all the bases of obvious African-American choice. Though the women characters were rather one-note, Singleton had a real grasp of story and, in the person of father Furious Styles, Singleton had created the Afrocentric father fantasy cinema.

I met Singleton in L.A.'s then-hot Roxbury's and in the subdued lighting of the restaurant all I could really see were big glasses, a baseball cap, and a baseball jacket. In the post–*She's Gotta Have It* era, John's pseudo-Spike look was extremely popular among bookish college-age brothers. There was great intensity radiating from behind those glasses and a cockiness that reminded me of a rap star. Listening to him talk so confidently about his future and snapping so disdainfully on several black film elders, I realized the hip-hop age of black cinema was under way. John, with his blend of nerdy knowledge and street affinity, was a harbinger of the future. Youth is a prevailing theme of this era of black film because the young filmmakers are obsessed with writing about themselves and how they see the world.

John's goals weren't at all inhibited by his race or age. Visions of moguldom danced in his head. He talked lovingly about the work of Spielberg and Lucas, and about the empires they'd built. He was well aware of the clout his agents at Creative Artists Agency wielded in Hollywood and he was determined to have their big sticks swung to his advantage.

When *Boyz* was in preproduction, I visited the production offices one day with Larry Fishburne, who'd agreed to play Furious Styles. The offices were on Degnan near Crenshaw in Marla Gibbs's Crossroads Arts Academy complex and around the corner from the Comedy Act Theater where Robin Harris ruled. That day I met John's producer, Steve Nicolaides, and John's assistant, Melissa Maxwell. Later, as Larry gave me a guided tour of the Crenshaw area, including the tough housing development called "the Jungle," we talked at length about the differences and similarities between Spike and John. In terms of script structure, John had already demonstrated an understanding of classical structure that Spike hadn't. The lingering question was whether he'd have the cinematic chops to realize his powerhouse script.

Aside from playing Furious Styles, Larry was excited about acting opposite Angela Bassett, star of August Wilson's *Joe Turner's Come and Gone*. It turned out that *Boyz* only hinted at their superb on-screen chemistry.

Compared to Spike, who is distant to on-set visitors, and Reggie, who's friendly but preoccupied, John's calmness was a surprise. There were lots of black folks on the crew and a generally laid-back atmosphere. The presence of Ice Cube was, in the context of 1991, a shrewd bit of casting. He'd made a loud, nasty exit from the Beatles of gangster rap, Niggas with Attitude, aka N.W.A., and then, with the aid of Public Enemy's Bomb Squad production team, made one of rap's greatest albums, *AmeriKKKa's Most Wanted*. These events had made him hip-hop's icon of the moment, and his performance in *Boyz* rang full of his intelligence, humor, and credibility. As time would reveal, Ice Cube, like many of his peers, would weave himself into a rich tapestry of contradiction by embracing the moralistic Nation of Islam while hawking that destructive brew, St. Ides Premium malt liquor. That this was a truly human conflict between righteousness and commerce made it no easier to swallow. Before Cube's public persona grew more complicated, John's film caught a more simple view of the rapper on film like a butterfly under glass.

Boyz, more than any of the other 1991 films, was able to satisfy both young audiences and their parents. It lost none of its intensity in the translation to screen. Most black Americans could see themselves somewhere in this film. It wasn't simply a gangster film. It wasn't just a preachy "positive" film. There was a feeling of wholeness to *Boyz*, as it tried to embrace several African-American impulses—ghettocentricity, nationalism, moralism. This reach gave it the strength to overcome some bloody opening weekend violence. *Boyz* in no way glorified violence.

I'm not sure I can say the same about the trailer. Everybody involved with *Boyz* agreed to a trailer that, through its use of Ice Cube's music and violent images, created a hyped-up climate around the film that increased the chance of violence. *Boyz* the film did not encourage violence but critiqued it—*Boyz* the trailer put salesmanship over social responsibility.

John stood by it. The trailer opened the movie, he argued, and that was what it was supposed to do. My movie can't be held responsible for a real climate of violence that exists in the community and was created by white racism, he felt. His argument had merits but his answer still bothered me. Too often the makers of black art want to take credit for the positive impact of their work but, when something negative is associated with it, white racism is an easy scapegoat. Self-criticism is not a big part of the current youth culture.

Talkin' Dirty After Dark (New Line)

This Topper Carew–directed feature was and is a disaster. It had a great premise—life backstage at a black comedy club. Despite the presence of Martin Lawrence and folks funny in other movies (e.g., Tiny Lister, John Witherspoon), the laughs were few and far between. The film opened only in a few predominately black cities.

Considering how amusing Martin usually is on film and on television, *Talkin' Dirty*'s overall lack of humor remains perplexing.

Hangin' with the Homeboys (New Line)

This small, well-intentioned film about four guys—two Puerto Rican, two black—going out on a Friday was touted as part of the black film movement when it should have been promoted as a breakthrough Hispanic film. Bronx-based director-writer Joe Vasquez was more insightful about New York's Latin culture and its intersection with black culture than he was with his two black characters. Unfortunately the film was a 'tweener. It wasn't as ambitious as an art film; it wasn't b-boy enough to be a street flick; it wasn't a comedy and it wasn't a drama. Matching two black males with two Puerto Rican brothers didn't seem to get at any particular theme or speak to any one audience. The two black protagonists were played by comics Doug E. Doug and Mario Joyner, but they seemed to have been constrained from ad-libbing. Too bad.

Up Against the Wall (African-American Images)

I'd spotted a microscopic ad for this film in *The Los Angeles Times* so the Hudlins, Bill Stephney, and I cruised Hollywood Boulevard in search of it one Saturday afternoon. We felt dutybound to see one of the year's few truly independent African-American features. Directed by Ron (*Superfly*) O'Neal and dotted with TV faces (Marla Gibbs, Stoney Jackson), it was billed as a black male coming-of-age story. The makers of the film were handling their own distribution and "bicycling" (moving a limited number of prints from city to city) the film around the country.

Wall was playing at a crappy triplex on Hollywood Boulevard. To get to the screening room showing it, we went through the lobby, out into an alley, and made a left into a small room. The popcorn was greasy, the room was small, the sound muddy, and the print marred by a bluish tint. We sat through about a half hour before electing to split. What we saw wasn't very impressive, but the condition of the theater certainly defeated any enjoyment we might have found in it. Shades of Pitkin Avenue.

This experience pointed out one of the biggest (and oldest) problems facing African-American filmmakers—the absence of quality theaters catering to the black community. There are a core of about six hundred theaters where the bulk of noncrossover black films generate the most revenue. These theaters are either in black areas or in downtown sections of big cities that whites don't frequent on weekends. Any cursory survey will reveal bad sound, crooked sightlines, and a slumlord's respect for maintenance. Black folk are not being paranoid when they talk about the slackening of city services in predominantly black areas. This is the cinematic version.

Whatever the merits or faults of *Wall*, it was a shame it had to be screened in such a shabby setting. But this kind of treatment isn't discriminating. The bigger-budget black films are subjected to the same unsavory environment and, more important, so are black film fans.

House Party 2 (New Line)

Following the commercial success of *New Jack City*, its producers, George Jackson and Doug McHenry, seemed determined to show that they were more than shrewd packagers, that they possessed artistic vision themselves ("vision" being a moviemaking buzzword like "leadership" is in politics). Originally slated only to produce New Line's follow-up to the Hudlin brothers' *House Party*, they fired video director Paris Barclay during preproduction and took control of the film. With *New Jack City*'s director of photography Francis Kenny setting the lights, they appeared poised to prove their point.

Unfortunately for these two very smart brothers, *House Party 2* didn't make their case. The film opened strongly (I saw it on Broadway and Ninety-eighth Street opening night with a packed house), but lacked the spirit and craft of the original and quickly petered out. George and Doug (and the two credited screenwriters) couldn't overcome one crucial problem: Robin Harris's absence. The ribald humorist who'd given *House Party* great ad-libs and a moral center as Kid's hardworking father, died of a heart attack in Chicago prior to production.

To some degree Harris's role as the film's comic star was filled by Martin Lawrence, who gave an inventive, engaging performance in this sequel. But the good values that Harris represented and that Reggie Hudlin had invested in the original script were sorely lacking here. Where *House Party* viewed teenage sex with a wink and wit, *House Party 2* was raw and over the top. Where music and dance were deftly woven into *House Party*, this follow-up fractured its narrative to force in unwieldy production numbers.

Strictly Business (Warner Bros.)

Described in the chapter titled "One Party=Three Pictures" in Part Three in excruciating detail.

During preproduction of *Strictly Business* there was a real philosophical struggle over the look of the female lead. The white producers wanted the light-skinned Halle Berry and the original direc-

Buppie Joseph C. Phillips and boho Halle Berry find romance in *Strictly Business*. (Courtesy of Warner Bros.)

tor wanted the darker-complexioned A. J. Johnson. Both were capable actresses and beautiful women. Johnson was hired and then let go during preproduction. Berry was finally given the job, though she remained vocally bitter about the color casting conflict even after the film's release.

Young Soul Rebels

This feature-film debut of longtime black Brit filmmaker and gay activist Isaac Julien was a murder mystery set in the London club scene. Julien painted a loose, happy picture of a multiracial, sexually liberated club world that's threatened by reactionary forces represented by a serial killer with a love/hate fascination with gays. Though its celebration of homosexuality put off closed-minded blacks on both sides of the Atlantic, Julien's touch was lighter and less didactic than his interviews would suggest. Julien, usually quite an avant-garde filmmaker, had recognized the need for storytelling in features and addressed it without sacrificing his politics.

True Identity (Touchstone)

Like Spike Lee, Reggie Hudlin, and Julie Dash, Charles Lane had paid his dues as a long-struggling indie filmmaker. In 1989 he made a beautiful little feature-length silent film called *Sidewalk Stories* that Island distributed. There was a gentle humor tempered by the realities of homelessness in *Sidewalk* that was a continuation of Lane's 1976 short *A Place in Time*.

When I heard he was going to make his first studio feature, I was happy. When I heard it was for Disney's Touchstone, I was sad. If any studio in town seemed unlikely to understand contemporary African-American life, it was the folks in the mouse house. I knew Charles was in trouble when they cast black British TV star Lenny Henry as the lead. Henry is a British Bill Cosby, with a well-liked if broad brand of humor.

But Henry means nothing here. And, in fact, Touchstone passed on a major African-American talent like Damon Wayans in its search

Director Charles Lane and star Lenny Henry, in whiteface, during the filming of *True Identity*. Photo by Richard Cartwright. (Courtesy of Touchstone Pictures.)

for a black comic leading man. Combine Henry's low U.S. profile with yet another horrible poster (Touchstone probably thought it was being hip with the fake graffiti logo) and the gimmicky premise of a black man wearing white makeup to avoid Mafia hit men, and welcome to 1991's biggest black comedy failure.

Livin' Large (Samuel Goldwyn)

Bill Payne adapted Oscar Wilde's *Picture of Dorian Gray* concept to black folks and video. Instead of a portrait that changed the protagonist's age, in *Livin' Large* a black television reporter looks whiter on video the more distant he becomes from the black community. This wasn't a bad metaphor for the trials of a black person seeking mainstream success. Critic Vincent Canby gave it a glowing review in the *The New York Times* but, much like *Strictly Business* and *True Identity*, the film had no stars, no action, and an ugly one-sheet or poster (this was the most garish of the bunch). There were some good performances elicited under Michael Schultz's always amiable direction. Russell Simmons provided a Def Jam soundtrack, but *Livin' Large* came and went without attracting much notice.

Daughters of the Dust (Kino International)

For a few weeks in New York there was no tougher ticket in town than the one for Julie Dash's *Daughters of the Dust*. During its initial run at a small art house through its longer run at a multiplex, the film had a long spate of sellout crowds. Before an afternoon Knicks game I scooped up two tickets for the 6 P.M. show to make sure I got in after two futile attempts to see it. The audience that entered the lush landscape of Dash's vision was the kind you'd expect at a reading by Toni Morrison or Alice Walker. Adult women, with a sprinkling of adult men and teenaged girls. They often wore bits of kente cloth from Ghana, had dreaded or braided hair, and had a righteous air about them. Maybe there were Mary J. Blige–looking sisters in attendance at some showings, but every time I saw *Daughters* (which was three times), women of the previous description predominated. In a year when *Newsweek* had to ask on its cover, "Was Cleopatra Black?" and acknowledge the Afrocentric movement, *Daughters* provided for its audience a deeper, infinitely more complicated view of the links between Africa and the world.

As one of the few feature films by an African-American woman, it certainly deserved support, but that's not what drew me back. In looking at the women of the Peazant family, part of a community of New World Africans, the Gullah, living on South Carolina's Sea Islands at the turn of the century, Dash eschews traditional narrative for a poetic visual strategy that relies heavily on signifiers from throughout the African diaspora to communicate meaning. That strategy meant the film must be decoded as much as viewed, a significant departure from the way most American films are made, which is why *Daughters* got richer with repeat viewings. I still don't believe I understood the meaning of every image cinematographer Arthur Jafa captured, but I felt the film and moved into its rhythms as one does a particularly allusive dream. I say "Amen" to *Washington Post* critic Rita Kempley's rave review:

". . . this nonlinear film becomes visual poetry, a wedding of imagery and rhythm that connects oral tradition with the music video." The range of black skin tones lovingly displayed in *Daughters*, the naked beauty of the Sea Islands and the story-telling technique—the film is narrated by a yet-to-be-born baby girl—make this a unique contribution to the black film canon.

Part Five

CB4

1992–1993

1992

Juice, directed by Spike Lee's longtime cinematographer Ernest Dickerson, has a thin script. However, Dickerson's guiding hand is solid, the hip-hop score on point, and Tupac Shakur's dangerously bugged-out performance marks him as yet another rapper turned screen star. Dickerson also directed *Surviving the Game*. (Courtesy of New Line Cinema.)

Wesley Snipes goes on a mad acting binge that includes a co-starring role in *White Men Can't Jump*, the lead in the Kevin Hooks–helmed actioner *Passenger 57*, and playing a paraplegic in the artsy *The Waterdance*. Snipes goes on to make the lousy *Boiling Point*, *Rising Sun* with Sean Connery, *Demolition Man* with Sly Stallone, and *Sugar Hill*, written by *New Jack City* scribe Barry Michael Cooper. The schedule is hectic but lucrative. Snipes is soon clocking over $4 million per picture. Jim Brown never had it this good.

Spike Lee begins a series of weekly lectures at Harvard University arranged by Professor Henry Louis Gates called "Contemporary African-American Cinema." Outside the lecture hall the *Harvard Lampoon* is selling "Mo' Better Milk Duds" and handing out a fake syllabus that reads "Sponsored by Nike."

Based on the Robin Harris classic "Bebe's Kids" comedy routine, written by Reggie Hudlin and directed by black animator Bruce Smith, the children's film *Bebe's Kids* is both an artistic and commercial disappointment. The Hudlins allege that Paramount sabotaged the project.

- Bill Duke directs Larry Fishburne and Jeff Goldblum in the smart drug thriller *Deep Cover* that performs better in the United Kingdom than the United States.

- The BFF and Jackson/McHenry Co., in association with the American Film Institute, coordinate a conference in Los Angeles, "Breaking the Cycle: The Business of African-American Filmmaking in the '90s," that places studio heads in dialogue with black directors and producers.

- The crucial flaw of Spike Lee's *Malcolm X* is not of artistry but of time. Its three-hour-twenty-one-minute length, while not unusual for contemporary epics (e.g., *Dances with Wolves*, *JFK*), has an adverse effect on the film's ability to attract the young African-American audiences thought to be prime targets of Malcolm-mania. The interest in Malcolm that manifested itself in T-shirts, slogans, caps, and sales of the slain leader's autobiography seemed not to intensify, but peter out at the time of the film's release. Despite Spike's amazing publicity campaign and very public struggle for control of the film with its domestic distributor, Warner Bros., *Malcolm X* as event (as opposed to the film as art) doesn't catch fire. Its nearly $50 million domestic gross is even less than the Wesley Snipes action flick *Passenger 57*.

 While steering clear of some of *Malcolm X*'s more racially charged pronouncements and underplaying his relationship with Africa, Spike

Denzel Washington in his Oscar-nominated performance as Malcolm X. (Courtesy of Warner Bros.)

probably did his most mature directing job in chronicling the life of a man in constant transition. Playing a character whose life was never static, Denzel Washington gives a performance that is controlled, yet vulnerable. Washington is ably supported by Angela Bassett as his wife, Delroy Lindo as West Indian Archie, and Al Freeman Jr. as the Honorable Elijah Muhammad. Ernest Dickerson does another magnificent job as he color-codes the film to Malcolm's evolution. Designer Wynn Thomas and costumer Ruthe Carter (who was nominated for an Oscar) do tremendous work under a budget that was undersized for the film's epic sweep.

Boomerang. This Reggie Hudlin—directed feature is an engaging, often screamingly funny, look at a successful ladies' man coming to terms with love. In Eddie Murphy's most charming performance since *Coming to America*, the superstar brings a lot of his own off-screen transformation from playboy to husband/father to the piece. The supporting cast is exceptional with David Alan Grier, Martin Lawrence, Halle Berry, Chris Rock, Eartha Kitt, and Robin Givens in top form. As the film's de facto villain, Givens is manipulative, smart, and assured. In fact, *Boomerang*'s weakest moments occur during the second act when, for a time, Givens's control of Murphy loosens and she takes a secondary role. When Murphy and Givens go one-on-one for sexual domination, *Boomerang* is as smooth as the hit-laden L.A. Reid & Babyface soundtrack. Though it lacks the cinematic invention of *House Party*, Reggie's handling of the actors and the film's humor are in keeping with his low-budget debut. The final product is loved by a wide cross-section of African-Americans but disliked by many white critics.

Bill Duke and Thomas Carter direct white-themed features for Disney-affiliated film companies. Duke supervises *The Cemetery Club*, a film about widowed Jewish women, and Carter handles *Swing Kids*, released in 1993, a music-driven story about fans of big-band jazz in Nazi Germany. Both were commercial failures that received mixed-to-poor reviews.

Whoopi Goldberg finally confirms her status as a comedy headliner with *Sister Act*. Goldberg is winning as a lounge singer hiding out as a nun to escape a mobster. The mix of vintage black music, great supporting characters, and a very Eddie Murphyesque role earned Goldberg's movie $100 million plus at the box office. She then uses her clout to get Disney to distribute the controversial South African antiapartheid musical *Sarafina!*

Some of the same critics who disparaged *Boomerang* love *The Distinguished Gentleman*, Hollywood Pictures' vehicle for Eddie Murphy that has him as a con man who goes to Congress. Contrived in the Disney-Hollywood-Touchstone formula, it is a throwback to an old Murphy style that was as stale as day-old bread. As well received as it was by critics and the white film industry, that's how soundly it was rejected by black audiences.

The Bodyguard is castigated by critics of all colors, yet it works for audiences, particularly women of all colors. White-bread hero Kevin Costner is cast opposite neophyte actress Whitney Houston in a corny story with sentimental songs, and the pop star acquitted herself quite well as a singer stalked by a killer. There is real chemistry between Houston and Costner that has women talking back to the screen. They seem both to identify with and envy her. The question of color is never raised by the film. Perhaps the on-screen love affair works, not simply because it is romantic, but because in America a star of Houston's stature loses her racial identity for consumers. She is Whitney Houston pop icon, not Whitney Houston black girl. Also crucial to the film's success, and part of why it is easy for black men to hate *The Bodyguard*, is how easily black women imagine themselves in a love affair with Costner.

1993

Guelwaar, directed by Ousmane Sembène and set in Senegal, is a deceptively simple-sounding film. The title character, a anticolonialist firebrand and devout Christian, is murdered before the film begins and his body is mistakenly buried in a Muslim grave. This incident is the spark for a

Chris Elliott, Allen Payne, Deezer D, and Chris Rock (left to right) cut up in *CB4*. (Courtesy of Universal Pictures.)

132

Executive Sean Daniels
lobbies Bill Clinton for White
House screening for *CB4*.
(Courtesy of Sean Daniel.)

series of escalating conflicts within the village that articulates class, religious, and political battles that still rage throughout Africa. Guelwaar,
seen only in flashbacks, is a charismatic character whose rants against
Western aid seem to echo Sembène's own convictions. Sembène is
arguably the best director of African ancestry in the world.

- *CB4* is the number-one movie in America for one week, utilizing the
same promotional and marketing clout Universal would use for its summer success with *Jurassic Park*. (And if you believe that I have a lawn in
Central Park I'd like to interest you in.)

- Despite a who's who of hip-hop cameos, the script for *Who's the Man?*
was awful with a capital "A." Comic Bernie Mack stood out as a comical
barber.

- Black female filmmaker Leslie Harris gets her dream feature *Just
Another Girl on the I.R.T.* to theaters via indie distributor Miramax.

Directors Darnell
Martin (Columbia's *I
Like It Like That*) and
Leslie Harris
(Miramax's *Just
Another Girl on the
I.R.T.*) with the
author. (Courtesy of
Kim Weston.)

133

Mario Van Peebles's *Posse*, the first black Western since *Buck and the Preacher*, is entertaining but muddled. There are a few more close-ups of director-star Mario Van Peebles than is necessary but, as in *New Jack City*, he gets good performances out of his cast, particularly Charles Lane, Tone Loc, Big Daddy Kane, and Blair Underwood.

The twenty-year-old twins Allen and Albert Hughes make a masterful debut with *Menace II Society*. Like the young Scorsese, they depict the rituals and bonding of young criminals with affection and gore. Unlike the praise Scorsese's *Mean Sreets* generated, shining such an unflinching light on black criminality was as controversial as it is justified. The Hugheses are hip-hop generation filmmakers, yet they are much more influenced by De Palma's *Scarface* than by gangsta rap. The Twins' use of sound design to heighten dramatic tension is superb.

What's Love Got to Do with It? looks like a television movie about the musically dysfunctional family life of the legendary Ike and Tina Turner. Though Brian Gibson's direction is uninspired, this film is a superb vehicle for the acting talents of Angela Bassett and Laurence Fishburne. Bassett, an actress of great emotional depth, is superb as the fiery yet submissive rock diva. Fishburne gives a nuanced portrait of self-destructive evil that he never allows to fall into caricature. Both were nominated for Oscars for their inspired teamwork.

Whoopi Goldberg reportedly is paid $7 million to appear in *Sister Act 2*. She then uses her ever-enhancing power to get Touchstone to hire Bill Duke as director.

John Singleton's *Poetic Justice* debuts. Janet Jackson is given a seven-figure contract by Columbia to star as a poetry-writing beautician. The

Albert (left) and Allen Hughes,
the twin menaces 2 society.
(Courtesy of New Line Cinema.)

Laurence Fishburne and Angela Bassett in their Oscar-nominated performances in *What's Love Got to Do with It?* (Photo by D. Stevens. Courtesy of Touchstone Pictures.)

film is not nearly as self-assured or focused as *Boyz*, though Tupac Shakur is quite compelling as the mailman who falls for Janet's beautician. For all his off-screen, bad-boy activities, Tupac displays great sensitivity in the role.

Director-comic Robert Townsend's heart is definitely in the right place with the super-hero *The Meteor Man* but, again, black audiences fail to support him at the box office.

Spike Lee's Forty Acres and A Mule Filmworks makes a deal with Universal Studios to executive produce low-budget features, starting with *The Drop Squad*, a film about buppie deprogrammers, directed by BFF member and longtime indie filmmaker David Johnson.

Doug McHenry and George Jackson, the production team behind *New Jack City*, strike a deal with the new, well-financed indie Savoy Pictures that allows them to fund a slate of low-budget, black-themed films at their discretion. According to *Variety*, there are restrictions on budget (nothing over $6 million) and theme (no period films), but otherwise this is the closest thing to a black New Line that has yet existed.

Haile Gerima's *Sankofa* is a fiercely Afrocentric work by a Howard University professor with no tolerance for New Jack swingers, Hollywood filmmaking, Western colonialism, or Christianity. Mona, a model on location in Africa, falls back in time to slavery days where she's a house negress at a sugar plantation about to explode into a bloody insurrection. Using money obtained in Germany, Burkina Faso, and Ghana, Gerima has made the most artistically successful and politically provocative African-American feature since *Sweetback*.

THE WRITING AND THE DEAL

Chris Rock entered my life one night at the end of 1989. I'd been aware of him since he performed on Eddie Murphy's HBO "Uptown Comedy Express" in 1987. He'd then made an indelible impression on me (and lots of folks) with his Rib Man character in *I'm Gonna Git You Sucka*. Late one night a short while after that at the hip New York disco Nell's, we'd traded some comedy talk while ogling young ladies.

But this night's exchange would literally change the direction of my life. We had a mutual friend who suggested I meet with Chris about some movie idea he had. Anxious to get on her good side, I said "Sure." At this point working on someone else's idea wasn't really very appealing. Between *Def by Temptation*, *Strictly Business*, and my work on a book about black men in basketball, I was pretty stressed.

Chris's dream was beautifully simple: "I want to make a rap *Spinal Tap*." Rob Reiner's debut film had been a mock documentary on the ups and downs of a British heavy-metal quartet named "Spinal Tap." It was a wondrously full cult movie that managed to send up both rock and pompous documentaries about rock equally effectively. I'd loved it and was immediately excited by the prospects of working on something like it. I also knew that with its blend of commercialized rebellion and larger-than-life performers, hip-hop was ripe for parody. The problem was, Chris had nothing else.

He didn't know the group's name. He didn't know who the group members were. He didn't know where they were from or what style of rap they performed. And he had no story (this would be a problem from that first meeting right up to the last preview). I made a list of five questions for Chris to answer and showed him the door. Despite my admiration for his comic talent, I wasn't sure if Chris was really serious. I was already involved with a couple of troubled low-budget films and didn't need a third. I figured the next time I saw him would be in the back room at Nell's or at some concert.

To my surprise Chris called me within days with answers to all my questions: The group would be called Cell Block 4; the band members would be called Homicide, Man Slaughter, Stab Master Arson, and Dead Mike; they would be from Brooklyn; they would be based on some combination of Run-D.M.C. and N.W.A.; and the narrative would revolve around a British journalist trying to do a documentary on them. I loved all of it.

None of the rap-based films to date had captured the wild mix of machismo and youthful abandon that surrounded the music. I'd been covering rap's growth since I saw DJ Kool Herc in the Bronx back in 1978. Like soul singers, rappers celebrated the commonality of the black existence, something the calculated pop iconography of Michael Jackson and Lionel Richie had sacrificed for an often dubious universality. Rap was a very effective antidote to the urban contemporary crossover-consumed black music of the mid- to late seventies. It brought a street-corner edge back to the forefront of our music.

However, as rap evolved, its increasing glorification of black-on-black violence alarmed me. In January 1989 I'd helped organize the Stop the Violence Movement, a short-lived collective of rappers and young New York–based record people who'd made the cautionary gold single "Self-Destruction" and an accompanying music video and book aimed at younger people. The proceeds, over $600,000, went to the National Urban League. Yet I was painfully aware that N.W.A.'s subsequent "Straight Outta Compton" had redefined the rap game with its fat funk samples and gleeful nihilism. The neonationalism of Public Enemy was corroding into nihilistic gunplay. *CB4* seemed a great way to make this point without being preachy. It was well known that many of rap's so-called "street reporters" were actually middle-class kids whose records were as fueled by blaxploitation's flicks as real life.

Still, I knew we were walking into a cultural minefield. Despite African-Americans' innate love of good humor and wordplay, comedy has always been a tricky area for us. Often in the past we've viewed it as a way whites have perpetuated stereotypes or blacks have revealed sides of themselves that embarrassed the race. This has gone on since the days of burnt-cork blackface and continues on in these days of black faces before the camera. People forget that Richard Pryor was once routinely attacked for his scatological style. *In Living Color*, under its originator, Keenen Ivory Wayans, took plenty of abuse from whites and blacks even though it won an Emmy its first year. There was no question that *CB4*, even if we made it as bland as a McDonald's commercial, would get somebody mad. Hip-hop culture has legions ready to attack and defend it at the drop of a needle on vinyl. Now if we really joked about its machoism and sexism, as well as the cynical use of it as a straw man by neocons, we'd get somebody upset.

This already complicated situation would escalate if we made a deal with a Hollywood studio for the script. The minute that happens, the stakes are raised, and no matter what good intentions people go in with (or at least claim to), the project changes. You are guaranteed to see one fourth to one third of the original idea sacrificed to the great God of commerciality. In fact, if you manage to preserve that much, then you should consider yourself fortunate. All of this was troubling.

Still, I couldn't help being drawn in. I thought we could make money by reaching the young moviegoing audience who had ignored *Strictly Business,* while making fun of the ghettocentricity so many folks were buying into. This thinking, of course, led to a contradiction that haunted the film from start to finish: How do you make fun of something the majority of your audience will find appealing while still entertaining them and holding their interest? This was probably the central artistic struggle in making *CB4.*

Working with Chris, whom I viewed as a still emerging artistic talent, was too good an opportunity to pass up. Over the years I'd written about and befriended a lot of gifted folks. Now I was being offered the chance to collaborate with one of them. It seemed a fun chance to gamble on myself, something I've always enjoyed, and also test the limits of "positive" versus "negative" black imagery. How much creative freedom does a black artist have when torn between the demands of his financiers and the demands of black leadership for inspirational views of our existence in America? I'd written about others caught in this dilemma before and made judgments about them. Now I had a chance to ride this wild wave myself.

Chris's comic sensibility and my taste were surprisingly complementary. We both loved *Blazing Saddles, Airplane,* and *Annie Hall. Spinal Tap* was our obvious point of reference for *Cell Block 4,* but we actually spent more time watching *The Rutles*, a parody history of the Beatles, a collaboration between folks from "Saturday Night Live" and "Monty Python." It was a brilliantly droll work that featured Eric Idle as a BBC commentator and a slew of real pop stars (Mick Jagger, Paul Simon) commenting on the Rutles's fabricated career.

I'd written a lot of "serious" articles and books over the years, but working with Chris freed me to tap into my silly side. A bit of it had seeped into the *Strictly Business* script in a couple of spots. From the beginning we had an anything-goes spirit regarding *Cell Block 4*. All through the winter of 1990 into early 1991 Chris and I fell into routine. He'd stop by my house in the evening, we'd watch a comedy, kick around ideas with me taking notes.

Later we'd drive into the city where Chris would do stand-up at either Catch a Rising Star, the Comic Strip, or Harlem's Uptown Comedy Club. Then we'd retire to some diner in the Village or to Junior's in Brooklyn and kick around more ideas, occasionally writing stuff in crayon on Junior's disposal paper placemats. After spending years around the music business, the comedy world Chris introduced me to was a breath of fresh air.

Seasoned funny guys, like Colin Quinn and Mario Joyner, taught me how comics slowly develop material over a series of appearances. Catch and the Comic Strip were for Rock, Quinn, and the others, laboratories where ideas evolved into jokes and jokes into polished routines. What impressed me most about Chris's stand-up was that he was quite fearless when it came to material. I saw over the course of two or three weeks a throw-away line about an abortion rally evolve into a standard set piece about abortion, virginity, and the Supreme Court that he still uses three years later.

Though Chris was obviously influenced by Eddie Murphy, he was also quite steeped in the style of a then relatively little known comic named Jerry Seinfeld. To Chris, Seinfeld was the master of the joke for joke's sake. With machinelike precision Seinfeld executed his material. Set up, pay off; set up, pay off. In his head Chris was trying to synthesize the bawdy black comedy style that was heavy on sexual innuendo with the classic rapid-fire delivery of Seinfeld and the Jewish comedy school.

For every inside rap reference we'd write, Chris sought out a "big" jokey set piece that would be funny whether you liked rap or not. At the time we met the heat from Chris's HBO debut and *Sucka* appearance had cooled. A controversial appearance on *Arsenio Hall*, where an edgy "date rape" joke had resulted in Arsenio apologizing to his audience, had clouded Chris's future. He was making a good living working comedy clubs around the country but he was far from realizing his potential.

Things, however, were about to change. *New Jack City* was in preproduction in New York and Chris was being considered for the role of Pookie, a thief turned crackhead who plays a key role in Barry Michael Cooper's gritty script. While Pookie would at times serve as comic relief, he also had several important dramatic scenes in the film. In many ways the part was analogous to Richard Pryor's Piano Man in *Lady Sings the Blues*—a supporting character whose tragicomic life and death are sure audience pleasers.

With some smart ad-libs and real emotional stretching, Chris won the role. From April 1990 throughout that summer, I regularly visited the *New Jack City* set and hung out in Rock's honey wagon. It wasn't that these trips were very productive, since Chris was often tired and preoccupied. But the proximity to the set and the actors, particularly Allen Payne, whom we projected as our Afrocentric character Dead Mike, made our own project seem more doable.

That fall Chris's career got another major boost. He'd long wanted to follow in Eddie Murphy's footsteps and join the cast of "Saturday Night Live." Since Murphy's tenure, the only other significant black male cast member had been Damon Wayans. Wayans's early eighties tenure had been cut short when he clashed with Lorne Michaels on the interpretation of a sketch. Damon had, against the wishes of "SNL," given a character a gay spin. Since the show is live, it went on air. He was, reportedly, fired as soon as he stepped offstage.

Despite the show's traditional disinterest in African-Americans, Chris still wanted a shot. In the summer of '90 he was flown to Chicago to an "SNL" showcase, where he and other wannabe cast members auditioned. Late one night Chris called to say he'd been selected. Though in many ways Chris's three-year stint on "SNL" was frustrating for him, his increased visibility was an asset in generating interest in *Cell Block 4*.

Instead of being a vehicle for a good stand-up comedian, *CB4* was now a film for an "SNL" cast member with a big part in a highly commercial movie. That does not imply that we walked right into a deal. Nope. Using Chris's comedy contacts and the relationships I'd cultivated over the years at *Billboard*, we shuttled out to Los Angeles for meetings, meetings, and, oh yeah, lunch. Chris was with the William Morris Agency and an agent there thought *CB4* would make a nice cable special. No, it's a movie, we said. A friendly development executive at Tri-Star felt likewise. Finally the people at Irving Azoff's spanking-new Giant Records (the folks who'd so successfully marketed the *New Jack City* soundtrack) wanted to make it part of their development deal at Warner Bros., but the bunny people didn't get it. In fact, a lot of folks just didn't get it.

To clarify our approach, Darnell Martin, an NYU student, Spike Lee crew member, budding video director, and a friend of mine, agreed to direct a pseudodocumentary piece at the now defunct hip-hop club Quando. Darnell, who'd go on to direct her script *I Like It Like That* for Columbia, did a marvelous job cutting the piece into an amusing short. Everybody seemed to like it, but again the Warner Bros. people weren't convinced.

All the same, Chris and I were wedded to a fake documentary approach (aka "rapumentary") like *Spinal Tap*. We foolishly ignored the fact that for all its critical praise, that film made very little money and the Hollywood folks weren't convinced that the format would work as a feature. Everybody said what we'd written was funny; they just didn't think it was a movie. Chris and I were probably too stubborn on this issue. The script evolved over time—the rappers became West Coast hard-core, the white reporter became (a) white and (b) American, we created fake histories for the characters and a host of groupies, managers, and family. But we were slow to budge from the documentary approach and that was a mistake.

In L.A., I met a producer named Sean Daniel through Robert Christgau, my editor at the *Voice*. Years ago Sean had interned for Bob as a kid and they'd kept in touch. Daniel, I found out later, had been vice president of production at Universal for many years before leaving for a stint with David Geffen. Now he was back at Universal as a producer and looking for projects. I pitched him two

ideas, including *CB4*. Sean had started his studio career as the production executive on *Animal House* and was close to some of the
funniest guys in Hollywood (John Belushi, John Landis, Albert
Brooks). He totally got *CB4* and saw its comic potential. Moreover,
he was one of the few folks I've met in the film biz who seemed genuine. Things looked good. Alas, Universal bought the other idea and
passed on *CB4*.

Despite the fact that the idea was obvious and our script funny,
if admittedly chaotic, no one would give us the money to develop it.
We kept plugging away, adding scenes, characters, and gags.
Through the success of *New Jack City*, the shooting and release of
Strictly Business, and Chris's fighting for time on "SNL," neither of
us could go at it full throttle, but we kept taking meetings and zero-
ing in on an idea.

Chris was cast in a small supporting role in *Boomerang*, starring
his boy Eddie Murphy and produced and directed by mine, the
Hudlins. It was great to see these survivors of the black indie scene
hooked up with the world's biggest movie star who happened to be
black. Imagine Films, the home of Ron Howard and his producing
partner Brian Grazer, put the *Boomerang* deal together. Grazer, a
smart, self-conscious guy, got interested in doing a rap film. A dinner with Tone Loc had opened his eyes to the comic potential of the
genre. Sometime during *Boomerang*'s preproduction, both Eddie
and the Hudlins had mentioned our script.

One afternoon I got a call from Grazer, who'd read a draft. He
wanted to make a rap comedy. Were we interested? Sure. Could it
be PG-13? That's not what we wanted to make. Let's have a meeting,
he suggested. Out of loyalty to Sean I let him know about the call.
What I didn't know was the Hollywood etiquette of these things.
Apparently if a studio is offered a project by one producer, passes,
and then another producer successfully resubmits it, the original
producer can remain attached to the deal. This isn't a hard and fast
rule. But since Sean had such a strong relationship with Universal,
the deal came together with Imagine and Sean executive producing.

Within a matter of weeks *CB4* went from an unattached spec
script to a project with two powerful figures backing it and a deal
with Universal Pictures. It was quite a turnabout. Even stranger
was that I found myself in the position of producer. All along I'd

toyed with the title and the responsibility. But without the money to make the film or the clout to get it funded, calling myself a producer would have been a joke. Now I knew I had to protect myself. Chris was the project's star, but without demanding producer credit I was just a writer, the most disposable element in this deal. My attorney, Stephen Barnes, urged me to go for a solo producer credit. After all the bad choices I'd made after *She's Gotta Have It*, I should have the opportunity to mess up on my own.

Grazer is a consummate dealmaker. Using his string of successes with partner Ron Howard (*Splash*, *Cocoon*, etc.) as a base, Grazer had over the years gotten their Imagine Entertainment in business with Arnold Schwarzenegger (*Kindergarten Cop*), Tom Hanks (*The 'Burbs*), and Eddie Murphy (*Boomerang*). One key to Grazer's career is his curiosity. Not only is he constantly asking questions—sort of a Socratic approach to producing—but he goes out of his way to meet people who could provide the answers. He regularly sets up meetings with scientists, sky divers, diplomats, etc.—anyone who can fill a gap in his knowledge. He knows a little about a lot of subjects, some of which lead to movies, and he knows enough to sound interesting to any star he meets.

Grazer's attention span is short and his body small but wired. There's a kinetic energy to the man that reveals his restlessness. His ambition is, I suspect, fueled by his desire to make a mark separate from his much-loved partner. It must be hard to be constantly linked with a man America grew up with.

Throughout the production process I'd butt heads with Grazer's staff. I was trying to maintain my autonomy from what I perceived as bad ideas, while the staff of a very successful company was trying to insert traditional structure into our very wacky flick. The key creative advice we got from Grazer came during the script development process. He doesn't believe in "media jeopardy" in films. In our early drafts *CB4*'s comeuppance came through the public exposure that they weren't real gangsters but middle-class kids faking it. Grazer argued quite persuasively that some nasty magazine articles didn't constitute enough jeopardy to drive a movie, even a farce.

In response I came up with a character we named Gusto. I'd known a brother in New York with the same handle who'd hung around the record business before his murder in 1991. The real

Gusto was an engaging yet threatening bear of a man, a real mix of sly humor and danger. Those qualities were invested in Gusto and his presence gave the script actual jeopardy, a sense of physical danger and a nice way to contrast fake gangsters with real hustlers. Grazer's instincts on this issue were really sound.

Grazer's clout was essential in getting Universal to pick up *CB4*. No doubt about it. I learned quite a few lessons in power wielding by watching Imagine flex their muscles. But in the most intimate ways Sean Daniel remained *CB4*'s godfather. At the time Universal finally signed on, Sean was just getting his company off and running. He'd done one studio assignment already, *Pure Luck*, a forgettable comedy that he had put his stamp on by hiring Danny Glover as the costar with Martin Short and by giving the director's gig to an Australian female director, Nadia Tass. Though he couldn't save the script these hires give an indication of Sean's instincts.

He is open to the unconventional, the unorthodox, and the cutting edge. He hooked up with John Woo, the brilliant Hong Kong action director who'd be making his U.S. debut with the Jean-Claude Van Damme vehicle *Hard Target*, and with Richard Linklater, the director of the twentysomething cult-classic *Slacker*, who was to make his studio debut with *Dazed and Confused*, a day in the life of dope-smoking seventies youth. With *Field of Dreams* director Phil Alden Robinson, Sean was developing a movie about the Student Nonviolent Coordinating Committee's work in Mississippi during the civil rights movement. In either his director choices or subject matter, Sean's interest was as different from Brian Grazer's as Montana is from Sean's native Manhattan.

With his edgy aesthetic and music sensitivity (as a Universal executive he'd worked on *Animal House*, *The Blues Brothers*, and *Coal Miner's Daughter*), Sean totally understood what *CB4* could be as comedy and minimusical. Moreover, he rolled up his sleeves and got into the marrow of the film, doing everything from finding our able line producer Bill Fay to giving *CB4* office space in his Universal penthouse to spending many weekend hours sitting with Chris and me discussing humor. Sean always understood that *CB4* was joke-driven and his easy laughter always made us feel he understood what we were trying to do, not simply as a commercial businessman, but as a fan and, in the end, as a collaborator in our insanity.

During this early stage of the *CB4*-Universal relationship, one other person played a crucial role. Our attorney, Stephen Barnes, is a smart, calculating African-American from L.A. who works for the big Hollywood firm of Bloom, Dekom, Hergott, and Cook. Stephen is not the best-liked guy in town. Not that he's a bad guy—the man can be extremely charming—but he's methodical and, as clients like the Wayans clan and the Hudlin brothers can attest, he's always angling for that additional bit of leverage. The leverage in our case was to get Universal to agree to let the rights revert to us on March 15, 1992 (the Ides of March) if *CB4* wasn't in preproduction. Our goal was not to get caught in development hell—that dreaded state where scripts languish for years. Because Chris's availability was limited by his "SNL" schedule—he had four months off each summer—if Universal wasn't going to make the film in the summer of 1991 or 1992, we needed time to try to make a deal elsewhere. That bit of leverage would prove crucial.

From the time we were picked up by Universal in 1991 to the moment we got the green light in the spring of 1992, *CB4* had three directors and one false start, and Chris and I spent enough money at L.A.'s Mondrian Hotel to put a nice down payment on a house. I mention all that in one clump because all of these events are intertwined.

The director issue was, for me philosophically, the stickiest situation. As a longtime supporter of the BFF who believed in the need for more black directors, I wanted a black person behind the camera. But—and this "but" is crucial—I didn't want just any black director. That is to say there were black directors I wouldn't accept because either I didn't like their work or they didn't understand rap music. Yes, this was a black film. But it was more a rap film than a black one. And as some of the previous rap films had demonstrated, not all black directors had a grip on this world.

My list wasn't long. Reggie Hudlin was at the head, followed by Kevin Hooks, maybe Bill Duke, and a number of gifted but untested black video directors. Chris's emphasis wasn't on color but comedy. He wanted to look at either Ben Stiller, once a director of "SNL" comedy shorts, or Tamra Davis, a good friend of mine who'd done several funny music videos (Tone Loc's "Wild Thing" and "Funky

Cold Medina"), including Chris's comedy video "Your Mama's Got a Big Head." But in this phase of the selection process, Chris bowed to my agenda.

Reggie loved the project, but was knee-deep in preparing for *Boomerang*. Kevin was busy with *Passenger 57*, though he recommended another TV actor turned TV director, Eric Laneuville, whose agent told us he didn't want his first feature to be a movie his grandmother couldn't see. Chris and I met with Chuck Stone, a very talented guy who'd made clever use of animation and humor in videos for Public Enemy, Living Colour, and A Tribe Called Quest. But Chuck seemed offended by our intention to make fun of rap music, even affectionately.

Then, at the Hudlins' suggestion, we zeroed in on a bright young black Ivy League director-screenwriter who'd done a cute short that involved hip-hop culture and humor. That short also had a sentimental streak that Chris perceived as corniness. I brushed that worry aside, feeling that would be a good check on the script's possible excesses. This director's background, mixing hip-hop interest with high-brow intelligence, was as close as I was about to get to Reggie's unique blend. The director's first meetings with Sean and Imagine went spectacularly. CAA, which represented him, was giving us their blessing. My black film friends were patting me on the back.

But within the course of a couple of weeks it all fell apart. A meeting between the director and Brian Grazer was weird. The morning of our meeting Liz Smith's column in *The L.A. Times* contained a picture of Grazer and a long item about his wife serving him with divorce papers and accusing him of having an affair with Naomi Campbell(!). So if Brian seemed unusually antsy that afternoon, who could blame him? But my director was equally wired, rambling when he needed to be concise, evasive when he needed to be direct.

The last straw was a meeting at the Mondrian with Chris, line producer Bill Fay, the director, and me. It was billed as a general go-through-the-script, let's-look-at-the-budget gathering. It was really a can-all-of-us-work-together-in-harmony meeting. I had to know if, in my effort to be "correct," I was forcing the issue. About fifteen minutes in I knew I was when the director launched into a surreal talking jag about his vision of the opening credits.

In his polite way Bill started giving me a "Is this guy for real?" look while Chris slowly curled up in a ball. It wasn't long after that everyone agreed this talented young man just wasn't right for *CB4*.

With no director and rewrites continuing, we realistically couldn't start filming until spring 1992, at the end of the next season of "SNL." The disappointment and tension of this missed opportunity showed on my face. I woke up in L.A. one morning with a big hole in the right side of my beard. Hair had literally stopped growing in a spot about the size of a nickel. I'd had that beard since I was seventeen. Now I headed back to Brooklyn without a movie and without a beard. Crown Heights was exploding when I got back home. Blacks and Hasidic Jews were at each other's throats. David Dinkins was about to fatally wound his administration. *The New York Post* was spewing forth its usual divisive bile. Back to the real world.

That fall I made contact with two new Fort Greene filmmakers, director-writer Leslie Harris and producer Erwin Wilson, both of whom lived a few blocks from me. I'd known Erwin since he'd worked on several of Spike's early joints; he was a longtime local resident. Leslie was one serious and determined lady, and with Erwin's aid she'd shot twenty or so minutes of a black-and-white film titled *Just Another Girl on the I.R.T.* It was the simple story of a too-smart-for-her-own-good teenaged black girl who gets pregnant by a boy with a jeep in the fair city of Brooklyn. The subject matter—a black girl coming of age—was overdue. The approach was earnest. Most important, Leslie had that look I've seen so often in the iris of successful artists. It's a look that doesn't say, "I want to do." It's a look that announces, "I will do." She wanted to, no— excuse me—she was going to reshoot the whole movie in color in Fort Greene over the course of several upcoming weekends. Would I invest? Would I help her meet with some record people regarding the soundtrack?

Despite my own less than promising recent experiences, I quickly fell in. What can I say? I like confident artists. I gave her and Erwin a little of my ill-gotten *CB4* cash and a few phone numbers. Leslie and Erwin went about the hard business of shooting and finishing a feature film on a shoestring throughout the end of 1991 into 1992. Watching them work made me feel a little better about the *CB4* odyssey. I'd been where they were. I felt good about seeing how the studio system worked; I didn't feel like such an ignorant outsider. At the same time I envied how much control they'd have of their film. Success or failure, it was their baby to make. The financial and artistic risk of making a film like *Girl on the I.R.T.* is like a drug. It's gambling on your dreams—something I've always found exhilarating, and a quality I admire in others.

In the fall of 1991 Chris Rock got his wish. Ben Stiller agreed to direct *CB4*. Ben, a mild-mannered guy who respected good comedy writing, had no problem with our continued collaboration on the script. The son of the droll husband-and-wife comedy team of Ann Meara and Jerry Stiller, Ben was very influenced by the likes of Woody Allen and Albert Brooks. He believed in an understated, deadpan, nonsitcom style. Sitcoms, white or black, emphasize hitting the jokes with exclamation-point-hard deliveries, lots of big eye gestures, and very little wordplay. Ben also had a keen eye for pop culture parody; he didn't know rap well but he had a sense of what was funny about it. Later, Ben's philosophy and skills would win him an Emmy for his critically acclaimed skit show on Fox, "The Ben Stiller Show," and his debut film, *Reality Bites*, ironically at Universal.

The other significant event of the October-November period was our agreement to work with another comedy writer. My first choice was Pat Proft, who'd co-written *Hot Shots!*, the *Top Gun* parody which I'd enjoyed. There was a great comic love scene in that film involving Charlie Sheen and Valeria Golino and a sizzling sunny-side-up egg that inspired a scene which became *CB4*'s biggest laugh sequence.

Proft didn't work out. Bob LoCash did. He'd worked with the Zucker brothers (the makers of *Airplane)* for years, had contributed to both *Naked Gun*s, and had written the hilarious teaser ad for *Naked Gun* in which Leslie Nielsen and Priscilla Presley parodied *Ghost*. From our first Sunday afternoon phone call we'd all clicked. He told us that Universal and Imagine hoped he'd tame us. Instead Bob quickly showed he had an anachronistic streak that respected our craziness. Where Ben was into a comic approach that subtly stretched reality, Bob was always anxious to fracture reality. He had an almost vaudevillian love of gags and comic set pieces involving all manner of props.

While sitcom writers pump up reality to achieve a clumsy familiarity between audience and stars, in LoCash's Zuckervision, emotional identification was secondary to gags. Emotional investment meant nothing if a gag was not lurking somewhere nearby.

In essence, Ben's and Bob's comic visions were actually miles apart. Chris, depending on the joke, could go either way. His attitude was let's cherry-pick the best of both worlds. This is why the holiday season of 1991 will live forever in my mind. From the week before Christmas until the week after New Year's, Chris, Ben, Bob, his writing partner Jeff Wright, and yours truly spent much of that time cooped up in a suite at the Mondrian. Between Chris's "SNL" schedule, Ben's prep for his pilot, and Bob's work on a number of scripts, it was the only time everyone was free.

Talk about comedy school. LoCash brought a *Naked Gun* sensibility, Ben a droll style, Chris contributed his Richard Pryor meets Eddie Murphy pedigree, and I refereed many—and I mean many— disputes. I was basically the "no" man. I vetoed things I deemed too expensive, too crazy, or too far afield from the original *CB4* concept. Occasionally I got the vibe that Ben was using only half his brain since he was also working on his pilot when he wasn't with us. The man was working overtime. In my gut I had the feeling he wouldn't be free if and when *CB4* got going.

From that general haze of jokes, room service, and male funk came many gags, small and large, created, rewritten, or abandoned. Ben wrote one of my favorite lines for Trustus Jones: "If you can't trust me, you can't Trustus." Chris seized on LoCash's name for our fictional California town. "Straight Outta LoCash" would be *CB4*'s first hit. With three cork boards filled with index cards (each set of acts color-coded) and lots of room service plates scattered about, LoCash's suite was quite a scene.

Sean, as always, was smart and helpful. The same cannot be said for some of the other people we dealt with. One of Imagine's reps came over, listened to our work, told us we'd been "jerking ourselves off," and announced she was off to Hawaii for the holidays. She'd be calling us from the beach. It was a low point in the script's progression and one of those moments of film-biz meanness I keep in my memory for reference whenever someone kisses my ass. Everything you heard about how this business views writers is true.

Christmas came. Chris and I had never been away from our families during the holidays. Seemed like everybody in the business was in either Hawaii or Aspen. Luckily, Bill Stephney, a good friend from New York and music supervisor on *Boomerang*, was also stuck out there for Christmas. So at least we had a partner in misery. The other great consolation was that Tamra Davis invited us over to her house for Christmas dinner. She and her husband, Mike Dee of the Beastie Boys, lived in the hilly neighborhood of Silver Lake, a place of cute homes clustered together and filled with young couples just starting out. We spent a grand old evening eating Tamra's quite tasty cooking, rifling through Mike's vinyl, and listening to Tamra's grandmother tell stories about her late husband. He'd been a comedy writer who wrote for many stage and film stars including Slappy White. Slappy White (and Nipsey Russell too) were names that always made Chris laugh. Something about them signified an intensely corny black comedy style.

New Year's Eve night we walked down Sunset from the Mondrian to the beginning of West Hollywood where Roxbury's and Carlos 'n' Charlie's nightclubs sit opposite each other. Roxbury had its usual crowd of Eurotrash and starlets, while Carlos 'n' Charlie's had a real black L.A. throwdown with folks from Crenshaw sporting their Saturday night best. We must have crisscrossed Sunset two or three times that night, bouncing between L.A. pop and L.A. funk. Somebody pulled the fire alarm around 4 A.M. at the hotel, a hectic start to the busiest year of my life.

We left town with a thick funny treatment. It was, without a doubt, the cleverest version of the script to date, since it both parodied *Spinal Tap* and *GoodFellas*. I don't know how it would have played with an audience, but it read hilariously. Alas, the people at Imagine and Universal didn't see it that way, and they came at us with a typically brilliant idea: let Bob LoCash write the script himself. He was a professional Hollywood screenwriter. He knew comedy, etc., etc.

Chris flipped. I wasn't too happy either. We all knew Bob wouldn't be able to write this movie alone. Bob knew it too. The problem was that several narrow minds involved in financing this enterprise didn't get it. The problem was that they weren't *supposed* to get it; if *they* did, then our *audience* probably wouldn't.

Our aces in the hole were (a) whatever he turned in we'd rewrite and (b) if they tried to hold us to this script, Chris would simply refuse to do it. In the long run if Bob's script didn't work, it could (I assured Chris it "would") put us back in control. Chris's view was that because he was the star-producer-writer we'd always have the last word. So we took the calculated risk. And we won. Bob is an excellent comedy writer but this subject was too far from his experience to write a good script about it solo. He knew that all along. To the credit of my troublesome financiers, they saw that when they read his solo script. Around this time Ben's show was picked up by Fox and he took himself off the picture.

CB4 was back at ground zero, but we'd actually come a long way. We had gusto. We had a theme—fake gangsta rappers and the stupidity of hardness in urban culture. We had an enhanced palate of comedy with the contributions of Stiller and LoCash. Plus we had another year of real-life rap outrage, including the breakup of N.W.A., to fuel the film.

One night in the spring of 1992 I gathered up the early drafts of the script, the treatment we'd all jammed on over Christmas, and some new notions Chris had and just started sewing it all together in a narrative. Aside from including into a lot of the best bits, I focused on working in the duality between Chris's rapper and gangsta Gusto. William Goldman wouldn't be jealous of the resulting script, but for the first time, the damn thing read like a movie. Imagine and Universal agreed. Mondrian, is my room ready?

The director search began again. We talked to a lot of white comedy directors. We talked to several black directors with TV backgrounds. Talking with Charles Lane was enjoyable, but we felt his sensibility was too gentle for *CB4*. We didn't talk to Matty Rich, not because we didn't try but because he stood us up for two appointments.

It finally came down to my old friend Tamra Davis and a veteran white video director, Rupert Wainwright, who'd actually done more historic rap videos than Tamra. He'd worked with N.W.A. and Hammer and had the funny stories to prove it. I didn't like him. I wanted Tamra. What I realized was that Tamra, despite making an impressive super-low-budget feature, *Guncrazy* with Drew Barrymore, was facing an age-old problem: She was a girl. While there was one woman from Imagine involved in the meetings, all the others were white men except for Chris and me. Tamra is a slight, pale blonde who wore loose-fitting hip-hop gear exclusively. Rupert was a burly, big-voiced take-charge kind of guy. In other words, he seemed more "directorial" and you could feel the white men in the room respond to that quality.

That's where we were when Chris and I flew to Los Angeles after Memorial Day 1992. This trip was it. "Saturday Night Live" was over for the season. Chris had four months off to do this movie. We both felt that if *CB4* didn't get made now, it would never get made. If it didn't happen now we'd just chalk it up to experience and go on to another script. It was time to shit or get off the pot.

I kept a diary from our return to Los Angeles to the beginning of principal photography. These excerpts capture, if nothing else, the never-ending anxiety in filmmaking, at least from the viewpoint of a rookie producer.

6-3-92

2 A.M.

All these meetings are but a prelude to more meetings. Even if tomorrow we all agree that one of our directing candidates is the one, there'll be more meetings with the studio before preproduction starts and then more meetings to crew and cast up. And all that will be squeezed around rewrites and location scouts, etc. I see a lot of long nights and a lot of human contact on the horizon.

10 P.M.

Today:

Chris and I told our Universal executive we'd go with Rupert Wainwright as director. I have my reservations but everyone else wants to go with him, including Chris, and we don't have much time to mess around.

Universal said they'd talk to Rupert's agent about his fee.

Chris and I looked at his cable movie *Dillinger*. It was well photographed but the acting was flat as a board. Very disappointing. It scared me.

I called Sean and told him about the film.

Our Universal rep tells us Rupert doesn't want to do *CB4* because he didn't want his first film to be so much like another (*Spinal Tap*) and the production would be very rushed.

This moves Tamra up into first position.

We see "Moe's World," a TV piece by Kevin Sullivan that is as nuanced and well acted as *Dillinger* wasn't. We set up a meeting with him for the afternoon. The Imagine people aren't high on him but his work is too solid to be ignored, especially after some of the other guys they suggested we see.

We drove out to the Slauson and Western swap meet to get two *CB4* caps made. Burned-out buildings decorated Western from Sunset to Slauson. At the intersection of Slauson and Western there were fire-damaged buildings on every corner.

Kevin Sullivan is great. He was strong on story and made some very intelligent critiques of the script. But he had no hip-hop sensibility and would have a very short time span to get one. I like him a lot but not for a film steeped in rap lore like *CB4*.

After more talk we all agree Tamra is the one.

6-5-92

I slept late for the first time all week. Talked with Martin Lawrence's manager Topper Carew about the comic playing Gusto. Topper thinks the scheduling conflicts can be worked out. (They couldn't be.) We'll meet next week to see if the schedule for his new sitcom is compatible with our shooting grid.

Talked with Ice Cube's Pat Charbonnet and his agent Michael Gruber about Ice Cube's soundtrack involvement. It'll be less than we originally suggested. They want to negotiate a deal and then farm out the lyrics to rappers he assigns. We'll see. (That didn't happen either.)

Lunched with Bill Stephney, Melissa Maxwell, and the indie filmmaker Lizzie Borden. Went to see *Patriot Games* with the Hughes brothers. A snoozer. Portland beat Chicago in game two of the NBA finals in overtime. Clyde Drexler sat on the bench with six fouls and Danny Ainge played a major role. On Monday the final word is expected on the budget and Tamra. Universal production head Casey Silver is taking her reel home with him for the weekend.

6-7-92

Played ball this afternoon with comics Adam Sandler, David Spade, Colin Quinn, and his brother Danny—who was damn good—and ate with them at Jerry's Deli on Ventura, at which Eazy-E has frequently been sighted.

Talked with Sean. Kid 'N' Play's *Class Act* is a bomb and may not make $4 million this weekend. He's a little worried that these poor numbers will give them an excuse not to green-light us. "We may be at Paramount by Friday," he joked. Paramount may actually be a better place for the movie but to move it there, at this late date, would be cumbersome and waste more precious time.

6-8-92

9:30 A.M.

Class Act made only $3.5 at 1,100 screens. Ouch.

11 A.M.

This is crazy. Casey Silver hadn't looked at Tamra's reel. A weekend wasted and everything is pushed back. They did say we could start negotiating with Tamra but, of course, that means nothing without the Universal green light.

According to Sean and Stephen, Universal has until the end of the business day Wednesday to green-light us. Any time between now and then the word could come down. If nothing happens by then, we are automatically free to take the project elsewhere, probably Paramount. Chris Rock is frustrated and pessimistic, and very upset over what he calls "nigger movie" budget nit-picking. Chris says making black films in Hollywood is like being in the Negro baseball leagues. They won't give blacks the money to compete on an equal footing with white films of similar substance and subject. I'm trying to stay calm, though deep inside my stomach is churning. Waiting on these motherfuckers is terribly, terribly tiring.

1:30 P.M.

Lunch with Stephen gives us some room for optimism. According to Universal's business affairs office if we can lock up Tamra Davis's deal this afternoon, maybe we'll get the green light this evening or tomorrow morning.

3:30 P.M.

Back at the hotel I talk with a Universal executive and get real disturbing news: there's a screening tonight of a "rap *Spinal Tap*" called *AK-47*. Chris gets fatalistic. "It sounds good," he says and, to the degree that it's a good title, he's right. We'd already dropped the *Spinal Tap* comparison ourselves, but if *AK-47* is finished and good it's definitely a problem. Similar title, similar theme. New Line could put it out next week. Or, worse, when *CB4* does.

Last winter a trilogy of black identity-crisis comedies (*True Identity, Livin' Large, Strictly Business*) came out in a row and never established identities separate from each other. Too many "rap *Spinal Tap*s" in a row—no matter how different in quality—would siphon off audience interest. I hate having to root against someone else's work but I hope *AK-47* shoots blanks.

6:15 P.M.

The AK-47 screening is canceled, which means one less thing to worry about. The phone's been ringing. Tamra Davis calls to let me know she still wants to do the flick despite the low salary. Her agent tells Tamra that Casey Silver loves her work. Stephen Barnes says he made the offer to Tamra's attorney, but he just found out Silver hasn't approved her, though he hasn't disapproved her either. Our Universal rep calls on the car phone to say that's true but it just means he's weighing all elements of the film before deciding. He adds the budget is still being looked at and questioned by the physical production department and that Bill Fay is answering their questions. Chris Rock gets a call from APA, who are trying to represent him, saying it doesn't look good for the film at Universal.

6:45 P.M.

Sean Daniel calls. It doesn't sound good. The tone in his voice says we're gonna have to take it to Paramount, though he doesn't say those words. He thinks we can move it and still shoot this summer.

7:10 P.M.

Sean Daniel calls back and says Casey Silver feels Universal should do this movie. He asked Sean Daniel whether Tamra Davis was the one and Sean co-signed her. Studio head Tom Pollack (aka "Oz" as Chris calls him) is taking the script home tonight to read it one more time. Casey Silver told Sean Daniel he thought things looked good but the final word remained with chairman Pollack.

8:30 P.M.

Chris and I drove across the long twisting length of Sunset Boulevard out to the Pacific Coast Highway and Gladstone's seafood restaurant. Looked at the ocean, ate lobster and shrimp, and ran into the singer Keith Washington, who's in *Poetic Justice*. Rolled down to the Santa Monica pier. We blew off a lot of hostility playing air hockey and shooting minihoops. We really needed to get away from the hotel and the bull of the deal.

6-9-92

Today I vowed not to linger over our predicament. I slept until 11:15, strategically cutting time off the day. Next I pulled out my index cards and spent most of the rest of my day writing notes for a film called *Uncle Bobby*. The first act flowed very well—so well it surprised me. Maybe this script stuff is getting easier.

Then to the phones. If *CB4* is going to be delayed and/or shifted it's time to let more people read it. Even if they don't buy it, the script is good enough to get us other work. Got an unexpected bonus when I called Chris Lee at Tri-Star—he's going to visit the set of *Poetic Justice*, do Chris and I wanna come?

We hooked up with Chris Lee at Sony Studios and rolled over to the set on Forty-third and Degnan off Crenshaw. They were shooting scenes at a beauty school near the Comedy Act Theatre and the Crossroads theater complex. It was a very relaxed set with plenty of sweet sisters working as crew and extras, and many hulking security guards from the 'hood.

John Singleton was real cool. We kicked lightweight conversation as he set up a shot with Janet Jackson. It was a simple shot and set up—Janet opens the trunk of her car, stuffs some wigs inside, and gets in. Janet looked chubby. Chris Rock said, "She looks like George Foreman with dreads." I wouldn't go that far but she certainly looked a lot rounder than in Herb Ritts's "Love Will Never Do Without You" video.

Back at the hotel we ran into Bill Stephney and then rolled out to Aunt Kizzy's in Marina Del Rey for a tasty soul food treat. Got back at 9:40 P.M., just in time to catch Paul Mooney at the Comedy

Store. My man was in rare form. His work is so aggressive and racially edgy that Mooney is the perfect anecdote to the Def Comedy jamming of black comedy. Bill Stephney, who's recording an LP with him, will do a great job marketing this guy.

Back at the hotel Sean left a message. "GOOD NEWS!"

YES!

The green light came at the premiere of *HouseSitter* where Sean, Brian Grazer, Casey Silver, and Tom Pollack finally all got together. Pollack, the great and powerful Oz, gave the nod. So we're in business. Chris and I stood on the terrace, more stunned than joyful, and looked out over L.A.

6-11-92

Doing deals out here is a mean business. I've already felt bad about two that I've made. I'm sure I'll feel bad about many more over the next two months. It's sad to have to pay these good people so little but, for the good of the overall project, I have no other choice. Is this what capitalism is all about? Paying as little as possible to people starving for opportunity has worked for capitalists throughout the world and seems to be what is happening on this movie.

Maybe I'm just too sensitive. As the producer, my job is to get the movie made for as little as possible, as quickly as possible, yet not skimp on quality. It can be done. But already I find myself flinching at the corners people are cutting to be down with *CB4*.

6-12-92

I'm on the redeye back to New York to pack my bags for this adventure in baby moguldom. In the air over America I'm caught in the space between my past and future. There was something so comforting being a full-time journalist-critic. You said your piece, got your opinion out there, and went to sleep with the comfort of saying, with only an editor between you and the public, exactly what you wanted. I was an autonomous entity working in a form that doesn't matter in mass-culture terms.

Now I'm a key member of a collaborative team on a movie that will reach more people in one day than have ever heard of my books. This fact messes with my mind. Making the transition from cultural arbiter to commercial creator hasn't been easy for me. So much of who I am has been tied up in being an analyst of trends that to be a participant has made me uneasy, nervous, and uncertain as to where I stand in the world.

Since I left *Billboard* in June of 1989 I've been seeking a new place to operate. For a time it was *The Village Voice*, then the basketball book. But *CB4* has already provided me with the most intense experiences I've had since my days in the music trade—and we haven't shot a frame yet. I sit in meetings with only my instincts to guide me. My past experiences have prepared me to ask questions and think analytically. They have not prepared me to read budgets, hire crew, schmooze with studio executives, and revise scripts on the run. Yet this is precisely what I'm doing. I am a rookie in a world of wily vets.

Of course, I didn't know much about being a music critic when I started. Just loved music and pushing a pen across a page, and stumbled on to it as a way to make a living doing both. As time went by I got good at it. Eventually I even got a touch pretentious about it and, not long after that, bored. The music business was (is) packed with boorish types. Most critics are an opinionated, nerdy lot. The music itself, be it made by beautiful ebony-skinned singers or anxious white college boys in ratty Converses, didn't surprise and haunt me anymore. Except for a few exceptional records (Anita Baker's and Tracy Chapman's Elektra debuts) it all sounded like "product" to me.

When I split *Billboard*, I went into a musical cold turkey that lasted into the fall. I began listening again but it was clear to me I could never again be a full-time music scribe. I've done a couple of fun things since then. However, nothing felt like it was the next move in my life. Because there's so much to learn about movies it'll be a long time before this producer-writer gig bores me. I never really learned the *Voice*'s word-processing system. It'd be nice if I learned to read a budget and started this career off right. *CB4* is an incredible chance to grow. I'm being paid to learn the game.

The most exciting part of the last few days has been the exhilaration of pulling all these pieces of the team together. It's not as internally satisfying as writing, but there is a desire to be part of a team, something larger than myself, with friends whose talent I respect, that energizes me.

6-12-92

9:35 P.M.

I'm watching one of my favorite films, Robert Altman's *Nashville*, on my first night back in Brooklyn. Altman used country music as a way to study America's values in the bicentennial year; we're looking at rap's role in American society circa 1993. Though very different in tone and outlook from *CB4*, *Nashville* has made me aware of how important audience reaction shots will be in articulating the band's impact on its listeners.

It makes me think of the issues related to translating black music to film. To take a bright high school MTV watcher and teach her to understand Otis Redding's "Try a Little Tenderness" as music and African-American culture is eminently doable. However, to instill a passion for it in her seems out of the question. She may yet acquire it for herself but training alone won't do it. So if under-twenty-five-year-old blacks don't want to support *The Five Heartbeats* or *Mo' Better Blues*, no amount of pleading, cajoling, or cultural guilt-tripping is going to make them. The musical narrowness of the contemporary African-American moviegoing audience weighed against those films. Yes, these were conceived, directed, and produced by black people, but these were black films that needed considerable white interest to balance the taste and age gap that separates young black customers from music that constitutes their heritage.

Still, watching *Carmen Jones* the other night on cable in L.A. made me want to do an all-black musical. I've been looking at old ideas I've had and came up with a couple of new ones involving music. However, I can't ignore the musical limitations of current audiences in sketching out any musical idea. Just because I love old soul and Robert Johnson's blues as well as hip-hop doesn't mean I can expect one audience to enjoy them all too. What is great black music to me doesn't necessarily register in the gut of this generation. I want to teach them about this music, as I have in my printed work, and I want to reach them, which in mass-culture terms is an uneasy balance. Without a way to draw them in you're just preaching to the converted.

6-13-92

Don't know how many Hollywood film producers ride the D train these days, but you can now count me in that select group. A Jewish grandfather sits next to me. A young brother in a crispy Avia parachute-material track suit squats next to him. A black mother holding a sleeping, open-mouthed seven-year-old garbed in Ninja Turtle power sneakers in one arm and her shopping bag in the other is on the other side of me.

There are scores of other scenes around me—stimulation overload that changes with every stop. This is why New York still pisses all over L.A. I get more ideas rolling from Houston Street to De Kalb Avenue on the D than I'd get in five trips down Sunset Boulevard. Each section of L.A. is so segregated that there's little up-front cultural interaction. It's there in L.A. but it doesn't announce itself and say, "Pay attention!" as it does here.

9:05 P.M.

The sun set a while ago but it's still light outside. From my living-room window I see a couple on motorcycles, two girls playing catch, mothers carrying babies, daddies smoking Kools, and little boys practicing their Kris Kross walk as they pass my house. It's Brooklyn, it's beautiful, but now my mind's back in Cali. I've packed two big bags of clothes, opened my pile of mail, and selected which folders stuffed with notes are staying. Now I'm ready to get this party started.

6-14-92

Can you be both a Berry Gordy mass-culture capitalist and a Ron Karenga–influenced cultural nationalist? What brings that bizarre question on? Leslie Harris's *Just Another Girl on the I.R.T.* was just purchased for distribution by Miramax. The same week we got the green light for *CB4* from Universal, Harvey Weinstein was negotiating with Leslie, her attorney Lisa Davis, and the producer's rep John Pierson. Weinstein, a very smart businessman, flipped for *Girl* as a film and marketing opportunity. It's a personal triumph for Leslie and her co-producer Erwin that the film's been picked up. They fought and they believed and now they'll get their day in court.

I feel like it confirms my instincts about the film's potential and my long-term dream of indie film financing for African-American film. As with Spike and, unfortunately, James Bond III, the need of black filmmakers to find money to complete their films hasn't abated. There's been a lot of publicity on black film, but the investors aren't coming out of the woodwork with cash. So the idea of using capital and media contacts to advance the careers of any filmmaker seems only right. Besides, it's fun.

6-21-92

Every artist's life is composed of two sides: moments of conception and moments of reception. You spend time creating work, then that work is displayed to others who may be collaborators, financiers, or just viewers. All of them, one way or the other, critique the work and, indirectly, the artist's creative process.

Having created and criticized both, it's clear to me the two are profoundly different processes. Criticism comes from the desire to dissect, pin down, and pull apart like a butterfly collector whose joy, is in the capture and mounting. It is the job of closing things in, trapping art in the critic's intellect. The creator must be open to all his thoughts, no matter what they are, and then sift through them to discover what elements of his random process deserve refinement. To be a critic is to be a microscope; to be a creator is to be an ocean that flows and ebbs and crashes. To be a creator is to maintain an expansive curiosity.

Major Trends To Watch: (1) Imagine's input. Will it be productive or will they attempt to throw their weight around? (2) Universal rep's slippery stances. Sometimes he uses "we" as "us" on the production; sometimes he uses "we" as Universal studio. (3) The budget. Bill Fay will get most of the flack if we go over budget, but it certainly wouldn't help my career either. (4) Crew chemistry: so far, so good. Nice, low-key hires so far. (5) Getting the music done on time. We're running behind because the Ice Cube negotiations went nowhere. We'll have to go with others. Maybe Daddy-O?

6-27-92

Sunday afternoons take forever in L.A. But this afternoon it was a pleasure. Had a publicity meeting that went very well. Cut my hair with hastily purchased emergency clippers. Bought a nice straw hat. Took a bubble bath. Listened to Eric Sadler's demo tracks for the *CB4* parodies and then spoke with him about the material. I ran into Dolores Robinson at the bookstore across from the Beverly Center, which is always a pleasure. The lady's so plugged in it's scary.

This week's big revelation was that I couldn't totally keep Universal's and Imagine's hands out of the cookie jar. There are just too many of them to attempt any containment strategy. They will have their say in various decisions. My goal now is to always be prepared when dealing with them, to make sure the production team and I always have our stories straight. As long as my side is in sync about the issues—from music clearances to cinematographer to unit publicist—they can't mess with us.

None of these studio folks are rocket scientists. They know more about standard operating procedures but my crew is expert in low-budget indie filmmaking, record production, comedy, and hip-hop sensibility. Our crew—competent and mellow—has hired other people down the line with the same qualities. We're only two weeks in—very early—but after my initial anxiety attack I feel things will be all right. All I have to do is stay focused for July and August, only two months out of my life, and the most time-consuming part will be over.

I've actually found an interesting place to walk on Saturday nights, a personal Sunset Strip that extends from the Mondrian

Hotel and the Comedy Store past La Cienega west on Sunset past Ben Frank's all-night luncheonette, the sidewalk cafes of Sunset Plaza, Book Soup, Tower Records, and the Roxy. On a lonely night you walk past rock 'n' rollers and bikers at Ben Frank's, trendy Eurotrash at Cravings in Sunset Plaza, Old Hollywood money at Le Dome and Spago, bookworms, CD junkies, and valley girls in spandex all seeking that most elusive of L.A. commodities—street buzz.

This strip of street life is enticing precisely because so much of this town's social life happens in stucco mid-city homes, seaside bungalows, and hilly canyons. In New York you do so many things in public in large part because private space is both costly and elusive; therefore, the idea of a night out being only hanging out at somebody's house is still a little weird to me. But I've adjusted or just learned to tolerate these rituals.

I've even come to terms with my weekend boredom. I used to loathe Sunday afternoons out here. All the East Coast ball games are over by 1 P.M. out here, and reading *The L.A. Times*, for all its sections, is still not an epic journey on par with the Sunday *Times* in New York (The book review section is so damn skinny). But Sunday nights in L.A. can be pretty cool—there's coffee shops like the Living Room where you can sip mint tea and play backgammon, floating clubs where you can dance, and the movie multiplexes are so relaxed you can duck into two or three theaters if so inclined.

L.A. reminds me more and more of New York. The weather and landscape are obviously night and day, but the racial tension, the traffic, the waves of undigested immigrants, the daily wrestling for power—on political and personal levels—and the often overwhelming sense that chaos is penny deep under the surface, all remind me of the Apple. Plus there are all these movies—*Boyz N the Hood*, *Lethal Weapon*, *Grand Canyon*—that posit L.A. as a city in brutal physical and moral decline. They remind me of that wave of New York movies (*Serpico*, *The French Connection*, *Superfly*) that, like Johnny Carson's anti–New York jokes, shaped the nation's nasty perception of my hometown.

Ever since I was a kid, New York has been detonating neighborhood by neighborhood, while L.A.'s recent critical mass sprung out of unresolvable class, not race, warfare. And I love that sense of being in a place where everything's breaking down.

6-28-92

So much of what I've written over the years has been giving "the black perspective." How much of a dodge has that been? Was the work a "black" perspective or a "Nelson George" perspective? Race can be a great explanation ("This happened to me because I was black"). It also can obscure and camouflage personality quirks. I've heard so many black folks blame missteps in their lives on "the system," "on whitey," on "the white man." It's as if they no longer have control over their lives and "the white world conspiracy" has bent them to their will. That posture gives a nameless, faceless white monster power over their psyche. It feeds into an impotence that can stifle the quest for excellence and self-expression. You can't ask white people to be good anymore—Dr. King got all we're gonna get out of that philosophy.

I see in *CB4* now not my desire to depict some example of black reality, but my glee in helping create a crazy burlesque of that reality. My writing on history tends to be pretty serious, but I actually see the world as a pretty wild place for which amusement is the only appropriate response. There's also a cynical streak in the script that's as much mine as Chris's. Where *Strictly Business* was a black fairy tale of empowerment, *CB4* is a nasty joke at the expense of street culture, conservatism, and extremism of various kinds.

7-2-92

As I've learned there are a million little administrative issues that crop up. Every bit of visual information that appears in front of that camera creates a paper trail—from the actors to any signs to the color of the walls—that some crew member, including yours truly, has to deal with.

Every description in the script raises a profound production issue. In the act of writing Chris and I had free reign. Whatever we thought of—crazy jokey inserts, scores of one-line characters—we worked in. We were ruled by what made us laugh.

Now as producers we've had to cut brutally things we loved. Characters and jokes that go back to our first meeting are eliminated with a simple X. As a writer it's tough on the ego; as a producer it's a joy to slash any unnecessary element.

With Tamra leading the way, Chris tossing in opinionated input, and the art department on a roll, a lot of issues are being handled by others. At first it was frightening to have things slip out of my hands. Now I'm extremely comfortable as long as I feel what's being done fits the original vision.

7-3-92

Mann's Chinese Theatre. Brandon Tartikoff and Paramount marketing and distribution chief Barry London meet Warrington and Reggie, Chris, Sean Daniel, myself, and a few other friends to go over *Boomerang*'s opening night numbers. Good news. Bad news. The film's made $5.1 million this Friday. Combined with the numbers since Wednesday, it's made $11.1 in three days. That's good. *Boomerang*, however, is only the number three movie behind *Batman Returns* (what else?) and (a shocker) *A League of Their Own*. The stats suggest that *League* has a "wide audience base" (read as white) and *Boomerang* has "a strong but narrow base" (read as black).

7-6-92

1. Bad day of casting: no excellent Virgil Robinsons or Davenports.

2. Major production problems with the schedule. Several scenes don't fit. Even if we went six-day weeks we can't get them all in. It's a big problem and I fear the loss of more funny bits in order to make this tight-ass schedule work.

7-7-92

Casey Silver spent most of a morning telling us how much trouble the IA union had caused a film about Bruce Lee (*Dragon*) now shooting in L.A. I got the feeling he liked our film's concept more than he liked the script, though he admitted he laughed out loud several times. He seemed both impressed and troubled that the film was smart, as if its wit would go over the heads of *CB4*'s young black and white core male audience.

The most positive part of the meeting was that in his mind this was Chris's and my baby. Not Brian Grazer's or Sean Daniel's. The film was being made by Universal because of *our* humor (Chris's), our musical knowledge (mine), and Chris's potential appeal. There was a real mandate in his words. If it fails it will be because we let it get away from us. Cool. That's absolutely true. If I have a big problem I can call him he assured me. But he (and I) both hope we don't have to speak again at the first preview.

There was a level of challenge in Silver's comments that rang in my head the rest of the day. Too smart. The unions. Our vision. The doubt I heard in his voice about the humor's mass accessibility and our ability to run the movie bounced around and around.

I actually love being the underdog. I was one in writing my first real book. To this day the experience of publishing *Where Did Our Love Go?* in spite of scores of doubters is one of the key events in my life. I feel real fired-up right now. The triumph of Berry Gordy still casts a shadow over the black entrepreneur who tries to fuse African-American talent and smart business practices to build an empire. That was true when I wrote about him in 1985 and still is. I understood his importance as a symbol of black business acumen as well as his more obvious legacy as a musical mentor.

But what's painfully clear now is how inadequate my understanding of the day-to-day processes of the creative businessman was. Watching Russell Simmons, Andre Harrell, and Spike Lee showed me how big a part of the job is harnessing the enthusiasm of young people, of convincing anxious, ambitious twenty-somethings to believe in your view of their talent and to follow your guidance. A man like Gordy had to be a teacher, a con man, a mentor, and a boss to scores of eager young people. With some you had to act hip; with others an air of paternal authority was essential.

At the same time he needed an administrative structure that pulled bright, young nonperformers into a union alongside older, white and black, executive-advisors. Harrell, Simmons, and Lee, like Gordy, have whites in important positions either inside their companies or as attorneys, accountants, or agents. These white men (for they are uniformly white males) give the blacks access to corridors of corporate power.

One of the harsh truths of American business for blacks, particularly those who work in concert with large white distribution entities, has been that all these young black entrepreneurs have had to make peace with the white power structure, one way or another. That is not to say that one must accept the artistic values of the white community—that is artistic death (see Gordy's Las Vegas fixation for evidence). But lacking the means of distribution and independent funding, these African-American minimoguls inevitably find themselves working with multinational white institutions that have traditionally remained hostile to sharing power with us.

So these middlemen liaisons are useful, but they can be dangerously untrustworthy. They can definitely be dukes of deception. The white executive/attorney/agent may for racial or, just as often, personal gain mess over or misdirect the black minimogul. As a result these relationships, even at their best, are always fraught with a subtle tension. These white middlemen are the unchanging same of the entertainment game. Gatekeepers, they flow from job to job, from trend to trend. The black minimogul tends to rise and fall on one or two creative ideas that, once exhausted, often send his or her career crashing down. At *Billboard* I wrote about many a "genius" who turned out to be a one-trick pony.

The genius of Berry Gordy was that his company was consistently evolving while remaining commercial. There were several waves of talent during the production-line glory years of 1963 to 1971. Even after the major corporations moved steadily after the black music market in the seventies, Motown still discovered important talent into the early eighties. Looking at this new black wave of businessmen, it's way too early to say whether Harrell, Simmons, or Lee will be able to sustain their importance for that long. For all their profitable activity I certainly couldn't say Def Jam, Uptown, or Forty Acres and A Mule has equaled Motown.

7-8-92

My longest day so far.

7:45 A.M.

Phone call with Bill Stephney in New York regarding the music sessions and his salary.

8:15 A.M.

Phone call with Leyla Turkkan regarding unit publicity involvement, her proposal to the studio, and hiring Cassandra Butcher as our P.R. consultant.

9:50 A.M.

On phone to various record companies (EMI, Jive) regarding the soundtrack while I write memos setting up the first read-through, recording schedule, public relations campaign, and getting the Ice Cube interview for film.

1 P.M.

Lunch with my attorney Stephen Barnes.

2:30 P.M.

Conference call with Bert Berman on the soundtrack deal, Bill Stephney's deal, hiring an attorney to negotiate the music fees, and Andre Harrell's possible involvement.

4:15 P.M.

Long meeting with Kim Hardin and Chris strategizing on casting negotiations with Nia Long, Rachel True, Khandi Alexander, Garrett Morris, and Willard Pugh. Talked about finding a big-name Virgil Robinson. Kim explained the dilemma of title cards. Who gets single and shared cards is a bigger negotiating point than I'd ever suspected. Line producer Bill Fay joined us. We talk about giving an "Introducing Charlie Murphy" credit to Eddie's older brother for playing Gusto. We schedule another 2 P.M. meeting tomorrow for further discussion. With our tight budget we don't have a lot of salary flexibility.

Got back to the hotel at 8 P.M. I read Walter Mosley's latest detective novel until 8:45. Went to sleep and didn't wake up until eight the next morning.

7-10-92

My afternoon meeting with Brian Grazer goes well. We discuss our philosophies, our lives, *CB4*, *Boomerang*, the Hudlins (he calls them "the Huds"), MCA corporate politics, racism, and women. He wants respect and consideration but won't impose himself. A good, necessary talk. I shouldn't be so defensive. We're making our movie, which is what we wanted. So I compromised and we rescheduled our Wednesday read-through from the afternoon to the morning to accommodate Brian.

Later Chris, Tamra, and I agreed on the *CB4* logo and made more script revisions. I continued on the music deals and Kim made offers to several actors. Had to tell my mother I can't come home next week.

7-12-92

2:23 A.M.

Being a boss sometimes pleases me. People pick up the phone or intercom when you call. They do their best to answer your questions quickly and, God willing, accurately. They smile at you at times you know they really don't want to.

The flip side is that you have to ask the right questions. People don't have time to do both your job and theirs. If you're not heads up, you can miss out on info you need to know. Lucky for me film crews are very self-sufficient. Production designers and casting directors know what they are supposed to do and how to do it.

The folks on the crew have made me produce by pressing me for answers to their million questions. Even if you didn't know what you thought a particular set or character should look like, by the time you've been grilled, you've figured it out. You say the wall is blue or the actor Chinese and, within the framework of the budget, they get you the best blue wall or Chinese actor they can find. The producer puts his mark on the production by who he hires from the director down, and how he addresses the numerous questions each scene raises (especially if he wrote the flick).

I'm impressed daily by the info Bill Fay, Kim Hardin, and all the department heads have packed in their mental Rolodexes. Still, it's equally clear that the script and the answers Chris and I give to these myriad questions define the production. To anyone who challenges our choice of director I submit they simply don't know how we're working on *CB4*. Because of the nature of the film and our history with it, Chris and I are defining the film's tone, though the visual texture and performances are Tamra's responsibility. And, without giving up any authority over those areas, Tamra's been very open to our input.

7-14-92

Today *CB4* got in gear. Al Payne, Deezer D, and Chris shot their fake LP covers and promotional material. They looked tough yet had a humorous edge. Al even got to take his shirt off in one pose that he was loving. Deezer was ninety minutes late—his car broke down and his friend's car broke down. I gave him a warning. Charlie Murphy was in the house and was reading well.

Kim Hardin, in give and take with the actors' agents, locked up Theresa Randle, Willard Pugh, Stoney Jackson, Rachel True, Glynn Turman, and Khandi Alexander with the input of Chris, Bill Fay, Sean and myself. Wanted Garrett Morris to play Baa Baa Ack but lost him to the Martin show and will try to replace him with Richard Gant.

Bill Stephney's deal was made—got him main title card in the opening credits. Eric Sadler's deal for music is coming along and the clearances appear to be in good shape.

Got the nod of approval on Set to Run/Cassandra Butcher proposal from Stu Zakim and Imagine's Michael Rosenberg. So negotiations with Set to Run will commence—Cassandra and Jasmine Vega will come over for a meeting Thursday.

Andre Harrell wants to come over tomorrow. Russell will stop by when he hits town next week. Finally got the soundtrack proposal from Stephen Barnes. Ran into Flavor Flav in the hotel lobby and, later, broke bread with record producer Sylvia Rhone and movie producer Shelby Stone.

7-16-92

11 A.M.

Cassandra Butcher and Jasmine Vega really pushed for an EPK kit (a promotional infomercial/featurette). I agree but it's not in our budget. Showed them stills from the LP cover photo shoot and introduced them around. They start on Monday, July 20.

1:30 P.M.

Chris, Tamra, and I went through the script and made significant cuts in the beginning. We even cut Baa Baa Ack's introduction, which goes back to draft one, because it would save us a half-day of shooting and things are still tight.

The rest of the afternoon Tamra and Chris worked with Rachel and Theresa. Rachel and Chris really pumped a lot of life into their opening scene by really getting physical with each other—kissing, fondling, and then pushing away from each other. The kissing was Rachel's idea. She's really thought through how to make the character's interaction with Chris real. With Theresa it was a matter of fine-tuning the comic beats but overall she's got it down.

Major drama over the music deals. The music attorney Universal recommended didn't fax Eric's contract to New York until 7 P.M. Contract! We'd asked him to send a deal memo. Then Eric's rep, apparently pissed, came back with an outrageous response—we commit to Eric's producing eight cuts on the soundtrack and cap his studio time for scoring to two weeks! I wasn't going for it.

So only Daddy-O and Bill are coming out tomorrow. We'll continue to negotiate with Eric but I'm beginning to think we may need to look elsewhere for scoring.

Went to see P-Funk at the Oasis (used to be the Palladium). Hudlins in the house. Eddie Murphy too.

7-17-92

12:43 A.M.

I'm in a recording studio. Daddy-O is seeking out drum beats from his vast catalogue. Bill is on the phone. Chris just split. The programmer and the engineer are pushing buttons. We've been laying down the tracks CB4 will "perform" on camera based on Eric's demos. But Eric isn't here and we don't have all the releases we need. All because of this slow-ass attorney Universal recommended. He gets sliced come Monday.

Bill and Daddy-O came in this afternoon and I've been rolling with them ever since. Our biggest disappointment is that Freedom Williams refused us permission to use any of the copyrights he's a co-writer on: C & C Music Factory's "Gonna Make You Sweat (Everybody Dance Now)" and "Here We Go, Let's Rock and Roll". The upside of that rejection is that Daddy-O and Bill were inspired to create our own hip-house parody for Wacky Dee. The track has the same tempo as "Sweat" but a different drum pattern and bass line.

Daddy-O is going to do the voice of Al (aka Dead Mike) but we still have no MC Gusto. We brought in a South Central rapper named Mann who had a bouffant hairdo, a decent DJ Quik-Eazy E. accent and a very indistinct delivery. Chris even tried to rap with hilariously bad results. Bill is gonna try to run down Hi-C tomorrow. If we can't get him we might try it with Mann.

The plan for tomorrow is that we meet with the music attorney, talk with Hi-C's manager, and get our paperwork together for Kool Moe Dee, etc. Hopefully we'll get any rhymes we need rewritten and arranged. Then Sunday we go back in at noon.

7-18-92

Spent two very surreal hours at the music attorney's Brentwood office. Bill Stephney sat while this man gestured erratically, displayed great insight, and spoke in an unrelenting staccato pattern that was interrupted only by our questions and statements. I don't know if he has a drug problem but there was a hint of alcohol on his breath. Maybe that doesn't indict him but Bill and I were searching for any explanation for his behavior.

But the man knows his stuff. His experience in music deals is vast. He's worked at a major studio and a big label, so he clearly knows both sides of these issues. The concerns he had were genuine and revealed an agile mind.

But as impressive as he sounded one minute, that's how unfocused he was the next. Three times he told us we needed to have the single come out six weeks before the movie's release—one of several details he repeated to my growing impatience.

He followed us out in the hallway and was still talking as the elevator door closed. We started laughing so hard we both fell to the floor. Neither of us had ever been in the presence of such a mouth before—and Bill has worked with Chuck D.

7-20-92

Mary J. Blige's "You Remind Me" is the number one R & B single in *Billboard*, a song from the *Strictly Business* soundtrack. So Andre Harrell did put hits on the soundtrack album, but while he profits the movie flopped. He's definitely continued his roll musically and he's leveraged that into a major multimedia deal. With Jodeci and Mary J. Blige he's created a second wave of Uptown artists and, without a doubt, has assumed the mantle of the consistent, sonically distinctive black music that Philly International and Solar once held. At the same time, in the record biz unsound business practices are no roadblock to success. His office has always been chaos. But then Andre's genius has always been youthful chaos and that youth has brought Uptown an energy that's been translated into both rhythms and imagery that suit this era. "Sloppy," "inexperienced," and "undisciplined" have all been used accurately to describe the Uptown operation over the years. So have the words "trend-setting," "cutting-edge," and "fun."

The MCA corporation has embraced him and, in Mafia speak, he's a "made man." When I last saw Andre he was coming from a meeting with Sid Sheinberg and Tom Pollack earlier in the day.

Impressive. At the same time Andre is still very much a homey, one who believes in bringing kids off the street and letting them figure the business out along the way. To paraphrase Andre, "If they just graduated from high school, that qualifies them to work at Uptown."

Where Berry Gordy brought children from Detroit elementary schools to listen to new Motown releases, Andre scoops young adults off black college campuses (particularly from Howard University) to make records and videos they'd want to see.

Back at the studio both Tamra and Sean advocated the recording of alternative versions of the more objectionable lyrics. I knew where they were coming from but it still peeved me. It shouldn't have—I know better than to have an ego about it—still it seemed like I was giving in on some artistic matter crucial to the black community. In reality it made good business and considerable artistic sense to have alternative versions of some of our fouler lines.

Tamra Davis and cinematographer Karl Walter Lindenlaub got into a debate with the studio over whether or not the "Straight Outta LoCash" video should be shot in black and white or in color and then have the color drained out later. Universal wants to do it in color so they can keep either option open. Tamra and Walter want to shoot in black and white because it'll look much better. A control issue—to be continued.

7-21-92

Conflict over *CB4* lyrics that started on Sunday continues. Sean is sweating me hard to get alternative lyrics written and Chris is very reluctant to write "clean" versions. He fears we'll lose the humor if we take the nastiness out of them. Daddy-O has, thankfully, been working on the lyrics and they seem to be coming together well. On Friday we get back together with Hi-C to complete his vocals. I cut "The Niggas, the Bitches, the 40s" out of the script because we won't have time to record it and decide to use "LoCash" twice in the film. Went over the wardrobe of Eve Edwards's character with costume designer Bernie White.

7-23-92

From 9:30 A.M. to until a little after noon, Sean, Bill, our accountant, and myself were in a budget meeting with four physical production executives from Universal. We sat there and went line by line through our budget. This is a process that every film goes through, but still it can be very intimidating. It's really a preaudit of a film's financial preparations and I've heard it can get nasty. But Andy Given, the guy assigned to our movie, is a sweetheart and is very happy to be working on a small, fun flick. I spoke to all questions regarding the prerecords and the overall music budget.

While we're meeting, a photo shoot goes on downstairs. The nasty magazine covers are being shot (Bernie found some women happy to do our seminude stuff) as well as family portraits of our principal actors for use in their homes. Al Payne was two and a half hours late, so we had to have a talk.

We got the rights to Run-D.M.C.'s "King of Rock" and agreed to take "Down with the King," a duet with Pete Rock and C. L. Smooth, in order to get the classic. (Profile would later block the use of "Down with the King.")

In the afternoon, Chris Rock, Al Payne, Deezer D, and our choreographer Jeannette Godoy (she did Sir Mix-A-Lot's "Baby Got Back") work at Regina's studio on La Brea. The Wackee Dee dancers, aka Sun and Shine, came later with her as well. I had to leave before Stoney Jackson, aka Wackee Dee, showed up.

Attorney Mark Diner seems pleased to take over the music contracts. He has lots of experience, which is great since he's going to have to play catchup on a lot of deals.

The bank changed completion bond companies today . . . two working days before shooting! Sean says it's not a problem and I've too much to worry about to let this bring me down. Universal tried to slip a clause into Sean's contract that demanded that *CB4* be brought in as a PG-13 film and he had to scream at them.

Stole a basketball from the prop department and bounced it around all day. It was good to have an outlet for all that nervous energy. No hoop in too long.

I got some script notes from Imagine. Most of them were

ridiculous and a couple were worth considering. I find myself digging my heels in on a lot of issues lately.

Talked with Al, Chris, Theresa, and Khandi about their characters and what they mean to the story. Because of the nature of the film their characters aren't well rounded, but more comic representations of real world folks. So the role of their characters in the satire, more than who they are, is more important.

7-25-93

Shooting starts tomorrow.

It hit me the other day that I've got very few friends in L.A. I've been in intimate contact with so many strangers. One day I meet them, the next day I spend long hours in their presence. Even the actors, with whom it's easy to fall into a false sense of familiarity, are in essence employees. We hire them. They do the job. We all move on and meet again at the premiere.

Hanging out with Reggie Hudlin after Chris's gig at Redondo Beach made me homesick. He reminded me of one Christmas Eve a few years ago when we went to the Fifty-seventh Street Playhouse to see *Sid and Nancy* and then went next door to the twenty-four-hour deli and just kicked it into X-mas Day as hookers, couples, and fellow insomniacs hung out. That memory made me depressed on two levels: one, it was just one of those great New York memories that no one who grew up going to malls will ever understand, and, two, it was a moment that Reg and I, our minds so pregnant with possibilities, will never experience the same way. We were egghead bachelors enjoying the big city in all its weirdness—a punk movie classic and deli food on the big Christian holiday. Now we sit in L.A. immersed in the movie biz, burdened with track records and the perceptions of others about who we are.

I always tell myself "Life is long." It's my way of guarding against hubris and self-hype. Yet sometimes I wish parts of it would go by in an eye blink, that the anguish of detail could be banished or at least experienced later as memory. Instead I have to go through the tedium and tension of this shoot. It'll be boring. Worst of all it'll be boring with bits of unexpected and unwanted panic. I wish it were September 15 and I were making my reservations for New York and then Virginia to see my mom and nieces.

The writing was cool and the marketing should be fun. But this process of capturing actors, actresses, and light on celluloid just seems like an invitation to anxiety that I would gladly refuse if I could. But I can't. In the words of Euripides Smalls, "So be it."

THE SHOOT

The daily diary ran out well before the movie's principal photography ended. Despite attempts along the way to pick it back up I was too busy to have much time for reflection. What I found in my notebooks were scattered comments to myself. Some were incoherent. No need for you to suffer those. But I found a few that suggest my state of mind.

On July 31 I wrote, "The dailies tonight were great! Chris Elliott has brought A. White to life just as we anticipated two years ago. He did 'My first drive-by' just as I've heard it in my head so many times before. Charlie Murphy's Gusto is the perfect parody of Nino Brown in *New Jack City*. Our costumer Bernie White has done a great job of creating a wonderfully stupid look for them. Al Payne was large in the 'Straight Outta LoCash' video footage. His lip synching was right on. Daddy-O's words flowed right out of his mouth. Chris and Deezer were comic, but Al gave the piece real b-boy flavor. I left the screening room pumped. I hugged Chris, punched the air, and in general babbled like a fool. Week one was a winner."

Quickly my euphoria was beaten down. At the end of the second week I scribbled, "Never have had to deal with so many people I don't like with no escape from them in sight. The days are long, the time for sleep fleeting, and the weekends more a prelude to the next week than a rest from the past one."

August 20: "My days are filled with meetings, plans for meetings, and monitoring the making of the movie. Exhilarated by the response to dailies and excited by the prospect of finishing production, my mind runs to the marketing and selling of *CB4*, to getting this multinational corporation working intelligently for it. Today we made, in principal, our deal with MCA records for the soundtrack. Today we had our first marketing meeting with the Universal staff and it went amazingly well. I told them *CB4* is a broad comedy in the style of the Zucker brothers and "In Living Color," attached to the subject matter familiar from *Do the Right Thing* or *New Jack City*. I tried to use successful analogies whenever possible. They listened intently to what Sean, Brian Grazer, and I said and asked no ignorant or racially insensitive questions. So far so good."

The last note was dated August 28, a Saturday afternoon. "Ten shooting days to go," I wrote, "and my body is sore. My nose is running. My arms and shoulders are aching. My energy-level meter is showing 3. Might have caught something riding on that trailer last night up and down Sepulveda Boulevard as they shot the scene of Charlie and Tyrone kidnapping Chris. I went from the set to the recording studio where we spent five hours laying down 'Rapper's Delight.' Then it was back to the set, playing the track for Al and riding on the trailer. Talked to Reggie Hudlin today. Then to Russell Simmons, who was in the Bahamas. It was great to hear their voices again. Reggie and I shared moviemaking tales. Rush offered me some Def Jam artists for the soundtrack."

Every day was damn near a novel. I suppose every shoot has its own variation. There were love affairs. Disagreements. Rewrites. Food. I weighed more during the filming than at any other time in my life. You get three squares a day on a movie shoot, plus all the snacks you can digest. My next movie won't be a musical. Running from the set to the studio and back was a killer. I missed the shooting of some key scenes because of it.

I really admired Tamra's stamina. She'd shoot all week and then visit Mike D. on the weekends at some Beastie Boys date. She was not letting work stand in the way of love. I still miss the camaraderie of the set. Charlie Murphy is a great storyteller. He's Eddie's older brother and, now having been around Charlie, I see he had a profound influence on his famous sibling. Charlie isn't the polished comic Eddie is (few are). But for pure storytelling I've never met anybody as good as Charlie. The brother's a black Spalding Gray.

We shot in a lot of dull, ugly places. Panorama City in the valley was 103 degrees outside and ten degrees hotter in the home we'd rented. It was just a horrid week. Chris seemed to disappear to skin and bones. We also shot a great deal of the film on Adams Boulevard where a lot of burning had taken place during the L.A. uprising. A lot of the city we saw just seemed naked, sad, and broken. It'll be years before many of the neighborhoods we saw will ever be rebuilt. Downtown L.A. is already built up, but probably should be torn down. To call the August air there unhealthy is like saying, "Yeah, Isaac Hayes is bald." We spent many afternoons breathing yellow haze. Inhaling that crap was easily one of the most dangerous things I've ever done. One day we shot a block away from the offices of "Rebuild L.A." in downtown L.A. and received some nervous looks from inside. I don't blame them since we were photographing a gun battle on the street next to them. We made sure we didn't get their logo in any of the shots, though the temptation was strong.

After all the smog and the heat and the long days, going to dailies was always a picnic. No matter what the working conditions were there were usually one or two funny bits that made them fun to watch. The dealmaking and the politics aside, it was great to see the script come to life night after night. What you realize is that nothing that happens on the set or between the people involved in making a film really matters. The only thing that counts is what goes inside that colorful rectangle.

POSTPRODUCTION AND THE SELL

I've noticed in most filmmaking journals that that wonderful period called "postproduction" or "post" is glossed over or ignored. That's probably because most of these books have been written by directors and not producers. What for directors a is very intense time spent alone with the editor, for producers is a time when you figure out how to sell the film, develop promotional tie-ins, and get your distributor to help you implement your ideas. Not a lot of yucks, but I had some of my most unadulterated fun during the six-month *CB4* "post."

The ending had always been a problem. We never had a great finish. Not when it was a documentary. Not in any of the other drafts. The ending we originally shot was a parody of *New Jack City*'s final scene in which a Harlem elder, played by Bill Cobbs, shoots Wesley Snipes's Nino Brown dead. In our script Albert Brown, Sr., portrayed by the fine Art Evans, saves his son from death at the hands of Charlie Murphy's evil Gusto. The difficulty was that Chris and I didn't study the model carefully enough.

In *New Jack City* there is a brief scene where Nino Brown threatens the old man that establishes a personal hostility that culminates in the shooting. No such scene existed in our script. So the ending joke didn't work, which, of all the bits to fall flat, was absolutely the worst to fail. In addition the audience reaction cards indicated viewers wanted to see Chris's character subdue Charlie. Even if the ending had been funnier there's a chance we still wouldn't have satisfied viewers.

Our artistic failure resulted in a tremendous tug-of-war between everyone involved. The newly-born asshole producer side of me, acquired during my stay in L.A., manifested itself. I was secretive. I was evasive. I shouted at and slammed the phone down on a Universal rep. I basically refused to talk to a rep from Imagine the rest of the way. The arrogance would have horrified my mother, but after three years with this project, I had little patience left.

My view was: If the movie's gonna fail, it'll fail because Chris and I messed up, not because we'd let someone else's jive idea kill the film. In December and January we did two reshoots and basically redid the film's last fifteen minutes. Tamra added one of the film's smartest jokes—the parody of Spike's moving-camera dolly shots. Chris added two of the sickest—an almost masturbation scene and the idea of dressing up as Sissy, the groupie, to trap Gusto.

Besides this additional footage, editor Earl Watson shortened "Rapper's Delight" and used it to segue into very slick closing credits that utilized some outtakes and some black and white second unit footage that I'd supervised. Earl tacked on Chris doing his Cheap Pete from *I'm Gonna Git You Sucka* opposite his partner from that original scene, Isaac Hayes, after the final credits. It was a piece that had been cut from the body of the film that we had decided to leave for the hard core. This ending wasn't perfect, but it was diverting.

The soundtrack helped ruin my second straight Christmas. I'd tried to avoid the chaotic negotiations I knew were inherent in soundtrack deals by getting proposals out to labels while we were still shooting. The first and firmest offer came from MCA Records, Universal's sister company.

They'd had a solid success with the *Juice* soundtrack and are located right across the street from Universal, which in theory made meetings easier. But even before making the deal I was warned by both Sean Daniel and Kathy Nelson, MCA's vice president for soundtracks, that the two companies had not worked well together in the past and some mutual suspicion existed between the two entities. Perhaps naively I saw this as an experiment in synergy. Could we get this whole MCA-Universal monster to work effectively for *CB4*?

In the long run it turned out well. We sold over 300,000 copies, not great, but all right. But the sales were not my chief barometer of the album's success. I believe MCA's marketing efforts for the soundtrack helped open the film. Using a technique they'd employed first for *Juice*, MCA sent out thousands of *CB4* promotional boxes to black radio, hip-hop shows, and, through a black video promotion company I'd recruited, local rap video shows around the country.

The boxes, stuffed with five twelve-inch singles of soundtrack music, *CB4* caps and T-shirts, a video of "Baby Be Mine" by

Blackstreet featuring Teddy Riley, and a trailer that generated lots of good will, lots of play at hip-hop radio (KRS-One's "Black Cop" was an immediate rap radio hit), and put the *CB4* logo out there well before the film's release. As an adjunct to Universal's efforts the soundtrack was quite successful.

That was the good news. The bad news was that the soundtrack fell victim to some of the very issues the film satirizes. After much negotiation and the help of a Danish record producer named Willer, aka Doctor Jam, we received the MC Ren track, "May Day on the Front Line," one of the most assured and angry post-L.A. riot records. Chris was ecstatic since getting a song by the ex-N.W.A. member for the soundtrack had long been one of his desires.

The basic story of "May Day on the Front Line" has Ren breaking black convicts out of prison to "give white people stormy weather." Cops, black and white, are shot during the narrative. The minute I heard the track I had two reactions: it was a dope record; it would cause trouble. MCA's music people projected it as the first single. I crossed my fingers and hoped we could slip it by.

Then, on January 27, 1993, Warner Bros. dropped Ice-T from the label. The pending release of his first post–"Cop Killer" music had led to irreconcilable differences between the rap star and the media corporation. In other words, they didn't want to face the conservative heat again—especially if it could endanger legislation in Congress designed to expand their cable operations.

The same day the Warner–Ice-T split was announced, someone in MCA's business affairs department finally decided to give "May Day" a close listen. All hell broke loose. Phones lit up. Faxes of the lyrics began flying around Universal City. The final decision about the record moved up the chain of command all the way to Sid Sheinberg, the president of MCA corporate. Sean had several conversations about the record with Sheinberg one hectic weekend. Thankfully the record wasn't dropped from the soundtrack, but it was emasculated. The antiwhite imagery was toned down, all obscenity removed, and this "clean" version was to be used for the video. On Ren's regular label, the independent company Priority, the record would have gone out as Ren cut it. In the wake of Ice-T's being dropped by Warner Bros., MCA was taking no chances.

The next battle was over Public Enemy's "Livin' in a Zoo." After some awful haggling with Sony and Def Jam, we'd obtained the track for the soundtrack. As an added treat, Chuck D and producer Hank Shocklee had recorded "The 13th Message," an impromptu state of hip-hop censorship speech that attacked MTV, black radio, Bill Clinton, and the most dissed woman in hip-hop, Tipper Gore.

Some members of MCA's black music department objected to its attack on black radio for not supporting rap. After one screening I was cornered by a member of that department who told me, with great vehemence, that if Public Enemy wanted to attack black radio they should do it on a Sony album. I credit MCA black music head Ernie Singleton for keeping "The 13th Message" on the album. "The 13th Message" was deleted from promotional copies sent to radio stations in deference to the black music department.

The final censorship issue involved KRS-One's "Black Cop." After extensive remixing, the ultra-articulate rapper had refurbished an unreleased track from an old album into a nasty dancehall track with a lyric contemptuous of black policemen worldwide. It wasn't a "Cop Killer" but it was quite derogatory. Well, some rack jobbers in the midwest (rack jobbers are the folks who control record distribution in chain stores like Sears) couldn't make the distinction. Some refused to stock the soundtrack with "Black Cop" on it. So a goodly number of albums were pressed up missing "Black Cop."

Much simpler was developing a grassroots campaign for *CB4* with moviegoers. We'd started back during production by printing up several hundred small postcards with *CB4* in white against a black background. On the back they had the names of the two Chrises (Rock and Elliott) and Al, plus the words "In the House. Spring '93." Through Set to Run's mailing list we sent them to writers, editors, and sundry other media folk with an interest in rap music. In the grand tradition of Spike Lee (he's been doing these postcardlike mailings since *She's Gotta Have It*), the cards generated a lot of early, inexpensive word of mouth. That was followed up with a color photo of Chris, Al, and Deezer D with the *CB4* logo across the bottom and more information on the back. Al's ample bare chest got the photo pinned up in offices across America.

During the period when we weren't sure whether Universal would green-light the film, one of the film's chief supporters was David Sameth, a vice president of marketing who was moving into development. He'd been a big champion of the film within the studio. Now he'd make a very tangible contribution. Using footage from the shoot's first three weeks, Sameth cut together a five-minute trailer that we showed to musicians, their managers, and record companies interested in being on the soundtrack. We also leaked copies of it to press people selected by Set to Run.

No one who saw Sameth's work wasn't impressed. Through kinetic, intelligent cutting, Sameth communicated *CB4*'s rude humor and enhanced it. Throughout postproduction, Sameth continued refining the material into R and PG-13 movie trailers, and into sixty-, thirty-, and ten-second spots. I watched Sameth's handiwork in theaters around L.A. and checked with friends around the country. With no big stars and little advance hype, Sameth's trailers made *CB4* stick out. When some trailers end, there is the loud silence of disinterest. I remember it well from *Strictly Business*. *CB4*'s appearance usually generated laughs or, at least, murmuring. The trailers didn't attempt to explain the plot—a useless exercise—but did what the best trailers do: communicate the film's spirit.

As did the one-sheet. A variety of illustrators, many of them black, were brought in by Universal to take a crack at it. Even Parliament-Funkadelic illustrator Pedro Bell did one. But from the pile of twenty-five or so approaches, I really wanted only one. That one sheet I saw one winter afternoon in Sameth's office is basically the one we used. The image of Chris in locks, jheri-curl wig, a wool cap, and a parental advisory sticker over his gold teeth was clean and lean. Any confusion about the movie's intentions was clarified by the word "comedy" superimposed on the parental advisory sticker, the list of comedy figures on top of the poster (Chris Rock, Chris Elliott, Phil Hartman), and the tag line "Sex, rap and family values?" Not a classic slogan but, again, simple and direct.

Our major conflict came when some factions wondered if this ad campaign would attract nonrap fans. There was a one sheet that on one side said "CB4" with the guys in regular clothes and on the other said "CB4" with them in gangsta gear. Chris was adamant that no images of the cast in their non-CB4 outfits be released to the media. He felt that the young rap-oriented audience reacted negatively to middle-class images. His evidence was *Livin' Large*: the same "before and after" campaign resulted in empty seats, and

Strictly Business, which had a prominent buppie figure on the one sheet and attracted empty popcorn boxes disguised as seats. What was funny about the film, Chris contended, was ghettocentricity being satirized. To go with an image that muddled the message was a mistake.

Like all our promotional imagery, the poster polarized viewers. Either it spoke to you as a member of the hip-hop nation or it alienated or even disgusted you. This niche-marketing concept is rarely employed at a behemoth like Universal, though for indies such as New Line and Miramax it's the key to their existence.

The final piece of the marketing puzzle was the release date. During the summer of 1992 it became clear from the buzz around town that 1993 was going to be a very competitive year when it came to the African-American audience. So I put my journalist's cap back on, hit the phones, called a friend at the *Hollywood Reporter*, and gathered up every scrap of info I could on films aimed at African-Americans and the youth audience. Then, with Sean's input, I drafted the following memo.

MCA INTEROFFICE MEMORANDUM

Date: September 21, 1992
To: Universal Pictures - Production, Marketing, Distribution
From: The Producers of *CB4* aka *CELL BLOCK 4*
Subject: Release Date And Marketplace Overview

CB4 has completed principal photography. What has emerged from the shoot is a very funny cutting-edge comedy that will have as its core audience a young predominantly male, multi-racial demographic. In planning the campaign to reach these very active culture consumers, we want to give you an overview of the current competition that will be going for a similar target audience and could block our exploitation of certain promotional outlets.

1993 begins with the following movies playing from the Christmas period: *Trespass* (Universal), *Malcolm X* (WB), Eddie Murphy's *Distinguished Gentleman* (Disney), Whitney Houston/Kevin Costner *Bodyguard* (WB).

Undated is a very low-budget pseudo rap documentary called *Niggas*

With Hats financed by ITC. There are no comedy or music personalities in the movie. This is a literal copy of the *Spinal Tap* format.

Of most concern is a New Line film starring *Yo, MTV Raps* hosts Dr. Dre and Ed Lover, and to be directed by that show's founding producer Ted Demme. It is scheduled to begin photography in October for April release. It's a comedy about the two stars as bumbling New York City cops and, according to our sources, has already reached out to several r&b/hip hop artists for appearances (including Uptown/MCA signees Heavy Dee, Mary J. Blige, Jodeci). They have also contacted CB4's unit publicity team, Set To Run, to handle publicity.

Whatever the quality of the New Line film it will have one major promotional advantage over us—MTV support. We contacted *Yo, MTV Raps* about promotional involvement in CB4 months ago and got the cold shoulder. Now we know why. Word is that MTV is planning a big spring break party promotion for the film to tie in with an Easter vacation release. Their post-production time would be tight and shooting in New York winter, as they plan to, is not easy. A delay in their schedule is possible, but whenever we decide to release *CB4*, this film could be a problem.

Currently, two competitive comedies are opening on Feb. 5: *National Lampoon's Loaded Weapon* (New Line), and *So I Married an Axe Murderer*, starring *Wayne's World* and *Saturday Night Live*'s Mike Myers (Tri Star).

On March 26, MGM has announced Robert Townsend's *Meteor Man*, a sci-fi comedy with Super Hero Townsend abetted with adult stars like Bill Cosby and some rappers in small roles. *Hotshots II* has been announced for Memorial Day weekend by Fox.

Action movies are competitive with our core audience: *Cliffhanger*, starring Stallone (Tri Star - Memorial Day weekend, possibly); *Last Action Hero*, with Schwarzenegger (Columbia) on June 18; Jean Claude Van Damme in *Pals* (Columbia); John Woo's *Hard Target* (Universal); *Beverly Hills Cop III*, if it gets shot and released by the summer; and *The Killers*, starring Denzel Washington and Richard Gere (Tri Star). Somewhere in 1993 is *Blood In, Blood Out* (Disney), as well. (Sean has some extra footage he is trying to sell them.) Far more than an action movie, *Jurassic Park* can have June 25 to itself, if that is the studio's date.

John Singleton's *Poetic Justice* is slated for mid-July by Columbia. Coming off an Academy Award nomination and with Janet Jackson, *Juice*'s breakout star Tupac and a slew of other rappers in tow, *Poetic* will have major appeal for both MTV, BET (Black Entertainment Television), and mainstream media. For any youth-oriented film opening near it, *Poetic* will be a major roadblock to promotion and publicity.

The ubiquitous Wesley Snipes shot a number of films in 1992 that will be appearing throughout 1993 (*Rising Sun*, with Sean Connery, for Fox, *Skeezers* for Beacon/Fox, and a film with Dennis Hopper). Because of his rising star any film top-lining Snipes will attract an active black audience.

Miramax has a low-budget black film, *Just Another Girl On The I.R.T.*, which they plan on positioning as a female *Straight Out of Brooklyn*.

The coming year is shaping up to be a very active one for films aimed at tapping the *New Jack City—Boyz N the Hood* market. If we wish to avoid a direct conflict with any of these films and be first in the market with our subject matter, then there is one ideal release date zone for *CB4*:

President's Day Weekend, (Feb. 12–14) thru early March. This is doable within our current production schedule, though obviously it would require an acceleration of that schedule and an immediate commitment of studio resources. MCA Records, home of our soundtrack, would have to be energized as well. An early opening would get us out before the New Line/*Yo, MTV Raps* film, giving us the market unencumbered and, as with *New Jack City* in 1991, we'd set the standard for the year. We'd be following the (hopefully) successful *Trespass* into the same theaters. (We also have cameos with that film's two stars, Ice-T and Ice Cube). Though our MTV involvement would still have to be worked out, the national music video request channel, The Box, has become a strong competitor for the active youth culture consumer dollar. The Box, with the necessary production dollars invested, along with a strong BET commitment (they've already done a set visit and aired a piece on the film), could help penetrate the youth/music marketplace for us.

An alternate plan would be to wait until August after most of the summer's big guns have been fired. With this date *CB4* would no longer be 1993's first movie tapping the rap culture. While we firmly believe our movie will be the funniest and most substantial of any of the comedies referred to above, our core audience would nonetheless have been approached and lured by other marketing efforts before such an August release date. This must be weighed carefully.

A decision on a release date would have to be made quickly if we wish to hit that February (or March) window.

Following that memo, Tom Pollack initially scheduled *CB4* for January 15 and the three-day Dr. Martin Luther King holiday. *CB4* wasn't quite the birthday gift I would have wanted for the civil rights leader, and thankfully the reshoots and concerns for visibility so soon after Christmas got it pushed back to March 12. Mike Myers's *Wayne's World* follow-up, *So I Married an Axe Murderer*, was slated by Tri-Star for that date. We worried that if Myers was a hit, the second week would be strong and siphon off any curious "Saturday Night Live" fans from Chris's lead debut. (Tri-Star later moved the film to the fall.)

The only film opening on March 12 turned out to be the low-budget sci-fi flick *Fire in the Sky* from Paramount. The battle for the number one spot that week would be waged between rap and sci-fi, between hip-hoppers and dweebs. I was sure we'd win, sure we'd be one of the rare black films to open atop the *Variety* chart. I also knew we wouldn't be there long. At my most optimistic I figured *CB4* might match *Do the Right Thing*'s $27 million or, at worst, *Juice*'s $22 million. The film was funny but its narrow subject matter and ill tone definitely worked against it.

The last real issue prior to the film's release was its rating. The MPAA gave *CB4* an NC-17 or X rating. We suspected that it was for the language but they don't tell you. How much it was related to the subject matter, we don't know. Universal appealed the ruling. Apparently the board was split 2–2 on whether *CB4* deserved an NC-17 or an R. Finally the head of the ratings board broke the tie in our favor. Though I'm sure Universal was nervous, Chris and I thought the ratings debate something of a compliment. Nothing like irritating the powers that be to make you feel good.

The reviews were all over the place, though I would say the majority were mixed to bad. *Variety* was the first review and it was typical: "Pic's appeal will be limited to fans well versed in 'Ice' etiquette, its reach blunted by juvenile humor and a scattered, disjointed narrative." Siskel and Ebert gave us two thumbs down with Siskel questioning our choice of rap music (so how many Geto Boys tapes do you have, Gene?). The *New York Times'* Janet Maslin said the film "promised sharper satire than it actually delivered" but had nice things to say about most of the cast, including Chris, whom she called "a game, confident performer with an I'll-try-anything approach to comedy." Michael Wilmington of *The Los Angeles*

Times, like many critics, complained that we abandoned the mocku-mentary format for a too-typical Hollywood structure. If there was one overriding criticism, it was that the critics, most of whom loved *Spinal Tap*, wanted us to continue in that vein. "One of the more adventurous of the recent African-American comedies," Wilmington wrote, "it still gets bogged down in those movie-movie formulas, those phony recipes for success."

The reviews didn't kill us, but they did kill any thoughts of crossover to an adult comedy audience. We'd have to rely on our own promotion to attract folks. Throughout February and March Chris and I traveled and talked about *CB4* till we were silly or dead. By the week of the movie's opening I was really dizzy but there was still more to do.

Monday, March 8, was the L.A. premiere with Fab Five Freddy and "Yo! MTV Raps" taping for a special *CB4* show that Friday night. Wednesday, March 10, was the Big Apple premiere done in conjunction with the Black Filmmaker Foundation. It was easily one of the best nights of my life with heroes ranging from Cornel West to Marley Marl in attendance. The next morning, March 11, I hopped a plane to L.A. for an appearance on "The Arsenio Hall Show" (Chris had done it on Monday). I'd been rough on Arsenio in my *Village Voice* column but Arsenio, who'd liked my basketball book, *Elevating the Game*, decided to have me on anyway.

After the show I caught the redeye back to New York. Back in Brooklyn Friday I slept most the day and then hooked up with the crew. Stretched across two limos were Chris, Al Payne and his girl Wendy, Deezer, Warrington and Reggie Hudlin, Daddy-O, Bill Stephney, and Sean Daniel. Unlike *Strictly Business* I didn't have to get drunk at the end of the night. Every theater was filled, though the quality of the viewing experience varied greatly from room to room.

At the Metropolitan on Fulton Street the room *CB4* played in was a disgrace. It was long and painfully narrow. There were speakers only in the front or those were the only ones that worked. Either way it was like viewing the movie from the ass end of a tun-nel. The image was far away and the sound was humble rumble.

At Twenty-third Street between Eighth and Ninth avenues, the theater was technically fine and the film played well to a predominately pepper crowd with a few touches of salt. But at the National Theater, where we'd held the premiere a few days before, *CB4* played with gusto. The main room was packed for the 10 P.M. show. It was our perfect crowd: black and Latino with hardly anyone over thirty in the house. One elderly black woman, who came by herself, was quite offended and stormed out midway through. When the sex scene came on the audience went crazy. People punched the air like at the Def Comedy Jam. It's probably as close to a slam dunk at the Garden as I'll ever come. We hit the Waverly in the Village before calling it a night. We made $3.3 million that night, more than any other movie in America. Sure the competition was only *Fire in the Sky* but we took it. I slept soundly.

The next morning, New York City was white. The biggest snowstorm of the century had ravaged the East Coast. People from Maine to Miami were snowbound. Southern cities like Atlanta and Memphis were blanketed. Sean kept me abreast of the race Saturday and through Sunday. *Fire* had pulled in front and, despite strong attendance for *CB4* in cities without snow like Houston and L.A., I went to sleep Sunday night resigned to second place.

Chris woke me up Monday morning with amazing news. He was calling from the green room of the "Live with Regis and Kathie Lee" show. *USA Today* had *CB4* listed as number one by the slim margin of $6.12 million to $6.11 earned by *Fire in the Sky*. Sunday is traditionally a big black moviegoing day (the theory goes that African-Americans tend to go out to clubs more than movies on Saturday nights). That pattern, combined with cabin fever among many folks snowed in on Saturday, gave us the edge. If there had been no snowstorm, we probably would have earned an additional couple of million and eventually ended up around $20 million.

It took me most of 1993 to truly recover from the *CB4* adventure. Nothing had quite drained me like the time it took to make this film. From beginning to end it was a struggle. And what was accomplished? I'm in no position to make any really objective judgments about its artistic worth. The reviews suggest it wasn't very good or, at least, was very flawed. I'd agree with the latter. The film hit a lot of targets, though not all as hard as I'd have liked. The ending could have been better. There was more cursing in the film than was necessary—if there was one single thing I could change in *CB4* it would be that, because it obscured the point of some scenes. All the same, I don't think *CB4* damaged the psyche of America, though it could have done a sharper job of strengthening it.

Still, as a fan of *Kentucky Fried Movie, Which Way Is Up?*, and *Blazing Saddles*, I thought *CB4* was often hilarious. It was a pleasure to watch Chris, along with Tamra, create so many gags on the spot. We also discovered a major acting talent in Khandi Alexander as the groupie Sissy. I learned more producing *CB4* than in all of my previous film experiences combined, and the film did well enough that Chris and I will likely get a chance to try again. That fact makes us survivors, if not winners, in the Hollywood system of compromise.

PHOTOS IN LONDON

The narrow streets of London's Soho teem with cabs, passenger cars, motorbikes, and cool-looking United Kingdom residents ogling each other from the sidewalk seats of sundry cafes. A spot of sun cuts through the morning haze, yet the city seems immune to warmth. London is a chilly town. Whether cool by nature (as in the weather) or nurture (as in the citizenry's well-documented reserve), folks here don't smile on the street and colorful clothing is hard to find. Even in the pubs, in which great jugs of beer are guzzled, laughter is fleeting.

Still a free trip anywhere is always fun. A free trip to London is excellent. A free trip to London to promote a movie is damn near unbelievable. Nine months after opening in the States, *CB4* reached twenty-five theaters in the U.K. the day after Thanksgiving. I've talked so much over here my throat is raw, yet I'm too exhilarated to give in to sickness. The unexpected journey of this crazy little movie continues on without a map.

On my last day in town I wandered through Soho in search of a little African-American warmth. Over near Piccadilly Square, at the Photographer's Gallery, there was a photo exhibit of Gordon Parks Sr.'s work from *Life* magazine. As weird as it was to be in England hawking a flick, it was even more bizarre to be viewing Parks's elegantly composed black-and-white images with British art students and the odd old lady hankering for her afternoon tea.

The most striking photos for me were a series from the fifties depicting devout women celebrating Christianity at a Chicago church. The shots are etched in a rainbow of grays and always exquisitely framed. Near those photos was a single image of an adolescent boy lying on his bed reading a book. Behind the bed, boy, and book is a huge crack in the wall, suggesting what squalor existed just outside the frame. It is an inspiring photo precisely because it communicates the thirst for knowledge that blossoms even in the most destructive environment. The photo drew me back to Brownsville, my family's life in the projects, and the dreams my mother instilled in me.

Marveling at Parks's work, I wondered how Parks reconciled

such profound visual poetry with directing several blaxploitation benchmarks. Between his photography, autobiographies, paintings, musical compositions, and all-around elegance, the eighty-one-year-old artist is one of the most accomplished Americans of this dying century. Yet to many he'll always be the man who made *Shaft* and whose son made *Superfly*.

From reviews from the early seventies, I know that Parks took some flack about *Shaft*. Some black folks yelled "Sellout!" as if that one work invalidated all his previous efforts or indicted his character. But this was the same man who'd written, scored, produced, and directed *The Learning Tree*, a poignant, now-forgotten autobiographical coming-of-age film set in his native Kansas, and who later made a sentimental, often evocative film biography of the seminal folk-blues songwriter, *Leadbelly*.

But even leather-clad Shaft himself, though sold as a sepia Sam Spade, was certainly some projection of Parks too. John Shaft was a freelance African-American businessman who lived in the bohemian Greenwich Village, did business on the bustling streets of Times Square, and stayed connected to the harsh heart of Harlem. Though filtered through the conventions of the genre, Shaft's existence echoed the range of Parks's own unconventional life.

Only an idiot would judge Parks's career solely on that film. The man's life is so rich it has already filled thirteen books. In contrast, when I look at the history of African-American filmmaking in the United States, I see a short story. The actual number of films made in the States that have been conceived and controlled by blacks is a pittance compared to those made by whites in and out of Hollywood. Even in 1991, "the year of black film," we represented a small, though noisy, genre.

Whatever the current perceptions of Spike Lee, the Hudlins, Leslie Harris, or myself, we've definitely not yet hit our peak. Many of the people mentioned in this book are so young (John Singleton, the Hughes brothers, Matty Rich) that we won't have a real handle on their talent at least until they're in their thirties. But even these directors, for all the hype, are not the point. In my eyes they are just the wave before the wave. They are the wave that sends a message that has young African-Americans putting down microphones and inputting script programs in their Macs. They are the wave that says the music of the visual will be accessible to African-Americans for generations to come.

Never have we had so many cinematic role models. Never have we had so many African-American film icons to be supported, challenged, and, yes, even overturned. Whatever rules Spike and company may have inadvertently laid down will likely be smashed by sharp-witted kids who consume videos like water. Kids will reject or endorse ghettocentricity or Afrocentricity or make up a "tricity" that speaks to their time. Just as Louis Armstrong begat Roy Eldridge, and Eldridge begat Dizzy Gillespie, and Gillespie begat Miles Davis on the trumpet, I see a lineage of possibility that might go from Oscar Micheaux to Melvin Van Peebles to Spike Lee to John Singleton to kids who'll grow up with holograph machines built into the bedpost. In short, the class of 1991's greatest legacy may not be the work it created collectively, but the "Yes I can" energy they represented.

This view may be too Pollyannaish for the cynical, not fixated enough in racial politics for the activist, or too distant in impact for the anxious. My reading of African-American cultural history shows us to be a people of great adaptability and ingenuity. It shows me that in our time of greatest peril we've never stopped growing. In light of our collective creative history, to predict anything but further innovation in African-American imagery is downright silly. Black film, at least as we know it now, is a baby with plenty of giant steps to come. Back out on the streets of London, I wander back to my hotel, living in the present, thinking about the past, but with my eye aimed squarely on the future.

Part Six

TWENTY-FIRST-CENTURY BLACK

1994

T I M E L I N E

1994

House Party 3 could have been subtitled *Kid 'N' Play Meets the Def Comedy Jam*. The genial rappers reprise their characters while supported by a slew of comics who reached national attention via the X-rated Russell Simmons—produced HBO broadcasts. Bernie Mack is again genuinely funny, appearing as the late Robin Harris's brother in a shrewd bit of casting, since Mack has assumed Harris's role as the down-home comic for hip-hop audiences.

New Jack City screenwriter Barry Michael Cooper made history by being the first African-American writer to have two films released in one year, *Sugar Hill* and *Above the Rim*. Both are set in Cooper's native Harlem and deal, as did *New Jack City*, with the insidious power of the drug trade in the black community. Unfortunately, neither is realized with the vigor of Cooper's first effort.

Sugar Hill is a gorgeously photographed but languidly paced portrait of a successful yet tortured drug kingpin, played by Wesley Snipes. In a decidedly introspective role, Snipes gives a controlled performance that plays against the vitality that made him a star. The film is stolen by Clarence Williams III as Snipes's doomed heroin-addicted father. The climax features a Hamlet-like bloodletting that more resolves than ends the story. *Sugar Hill* is thematically ambitious but, ultimately, falls well short of its goal.

Above the Rim, situated in the world of Harlem's legendary Rucker tournament, is about how much control drug dealers have over young inner-city athletes. It's a smart premise, but rookie director Jeff Pollack (best known as a producer of *The Fresh Prince of Bel Air*) can't balance Cooper's edgy aesthetic with his desire for sitcom patness. Tupac Shakur, the bad boy of black film, turns in another charismatic performance as the drug dealer Birdie. On-screen Shakur's eyes light up and dominate the frame. If he survives his twenties, Shakur could one day emerge as a true movie star. Not long after *Above the Rim* is released Shakur begins serving a thirty-month combination sentence of jail time and community service for attacking director Allen Hughes on the set of a music video. Their beef goes back to Shakur's dismissal from the cast of *Menace II Society*.

Matty Rich is a sloppy director. His second film, *The Inkwell*, set in Martha's Vineyard's black colony in the early seventies, proves that. Still, the story, originally penned by Trey Ellis and rewritten by Paris Qualles, is compelling. Larenz Tate, so frightening as O-Dog in *Menace*, plays a sweet, confused, nerdy kid coming of age in a refreshing view of African-American young manhood. Despite Rich's uneven direction, A. J. Johnson, Jada Pinkett, Morris Chestnut, and Joe Morton as Tate's father all do credible work. *Inkwell*, like most of this year's films, is a frustrating miss.

Spike Lee is a complex director. His seventh film, *Crooklyn*, set in a Brooklyn block in the early seventies, confirms that. The script, written by Lee along with his siblings Joie and Cinque about a family much like their own, kicks in with real emotional impact in the last reel. Before that the episodic plot is used as a vehicle for Spike's impressive directorial set pieces. The *Partridge Family* sequence involving the family's children is an instant classic. Yet the lack of narrative drive frustrates many viewers, and sometimes Spike's camera invention is too tricky for its own good.

The first black woman with a feature financed by a major studio, Darnell Martin, has her Columbia film *Blackout* (later renamed *I Like It Like That* by the studio) accepted by the Cannes Film Festival.

Actor Larenz Tate (left) and director Matty Rich on the set of *The Inkwell*. (Photo by Jim Bridges. Courtesy Buena Vista Pictures Distribution.)

Gordon Parks Sr., seminal figure in black film—and so much more. (Courtesy of *New York Daily News*.)

Denzel Washington and director Carl Franklin begin work on an adaptation of Walter Mosley's brilliant black detective novel *Devil in a Blue Dress*, hoping to turn the lead character, Easy Rawlins, into a franchise for Denzel.

Mario Van Peebles begins production on a film about the Black Panthers written by his father, Melvin.

Haile Gerima takes *Sankofa* around America, city by city, and plays to sellout audiences with the aid of word of mouth, black talk shows, and grass-roots marketing.

Following *Boomerang,* Eddie Murphy has retreated to his old comic persona. His Disney film *The Distinguished Gentleman* tried it and failed. So does *Beverly Hills Cop 3*. Director John Landis, fine with straight comedies, lazily manages the action, set at a theme park, while Murphy doesn't recapture the verve that made his earlier incarnations of Axel Foley so much fun. Murphy's next move? Re-doing Jerry Lewis's *The Nutty Professor*.

To the aspiring filmmaker Hollywood offers money, decades of technical expertise, plus marketing and distribution clout. The African-American filmmaker offers deep insight into his culture, vital nontraditional ideas about depicting America in general, and a built-in core of regular moviegoers. These differences can come together in some very complementary ways. Yet most often they don't. An intense struggle is waged over every black film that starts in the script stage, goes on during production, and flows right into marketing and promotion of the finished work. These battles pit the conventions of Hollywood craft ("how we do business") against the imperatives of even watered-down examples of African-American culture. Much of it is race. Most of it is class.

The thing I've found most striking about Hollywood as an institution is not its insensitivity to black culture (or Hispanic or Asian culture) but its misunderstanding of *any* subculture with an agenda or values that differ from Hollywood's obsession with the bland "universal" audience. Most people I've encountered in the Hollywood system exist in a cocoon of deals and dinners where decisions are based on what made money before and not any kind of life experience. Many of the power players were reared on TV and movies and attended elite colleges on either coast. Most have no sense of or respect for Grand Rapids, Michigan, or Rochester, New York, or Newport News, Virginia. Or whatever sense of felt life they brought to the job is eventually squeezed out by years of meetings, lunches, and screenings held within a very peculiar and insular world. Why would anyone expect them to understand that a good story is about working-class blacks or Hispanics, when these executives pay scant attention to the dramas of the white working class?

The people who control the motion picture industry (and television, too) in Cali live an existence defined by their time inside studio enclaves in Burbank or Studio City or Culver City, their time on a Los Angeles freeway to and from homes in Malibu or Bel Air or some really pricey resort. Within this narrow frame of human interaction they squeeze in test screenings, power dinners, and black-tie benefits. The car phone, the computer printout, and the formulas of hits past are the constants in their lives.

There are scattered African-Americans, Hispanics, and Asians living this lifestyle. But none have the juice to make a movie by themselves and they are in a constant and, basically, losing battle to maintain a nonwhite agenda in an environment where mass dollars are the only goal. They can be useful advocates. They can help another brother or sister out with advice or a little tip on the down low. In the record business, a black person affiliated with one of the multinational corporations can sign you, supervise your recording sessions, develop your marketing campaign, and, baby, make you a star. (In fact, if a black singer or rapper goes to a black entrepreneur with an independently distributed record label, the same process can occur.) Right now that process can't happen for any black filmmaker.

And I don't believe it will ever happen as freely within the film business structure. Some black executive may overcome prejudice and be so damn good at marketing or development that, like a Sylvia Rhone, president of Atlantic Records, or Ed Eckstine at Mercury Records, they are given the power to run a studio. But there are many African-American power players in the music business, both within corporations or affiliated with them through distribution deals. I don't see black film studio executives being granted the same level of autonomy.

My analysis will either be confirmed or proven false by two deals made in 1993. Spike Lee's Forty Acres and A Mule made an agreement with Universal Pictures to executive-produce low-budget films for the studio. The first, *The Drop Squad*, written and directed by rookie filmmaker David Johnson, was made for about $2 million. Veteran producers George Jackson and Doug McHenry signed with independently financed Savoy Pictures and were given a pool of money to greenlight low-budget black features with contemporary themes. Spike will be looked to for quirky art films that may or may not involve black characters and themes. Jackson and McHenry will likely continue to utilize the blend of urban culture and musicians as actors that have marked their work. Both these deals could one day evolve into the equivalent of record industry distribution deals. But, even if commercially successful, I still don't believe they'd address the need for more overall black control.

There will always be black filmmakers with deals at studios and there will be an increasing number of minority people hired by movie studios. But I believe the real energy of black film will continue to come from outside the mainstream, voices not easily digested by Eurocentric multimedia corporations. (Even the Japanese-owned media enterprises reflect an abiding Western cultural bias.)

The most politically potent African-American film of 1993 was Haile Gerima's *Sankofa*, a parable of a slave revolt that used African archetypes, a bitter anti-Christian attitude, and quite skillful storytelling to critique slavery and dramatize an argument for pan-African unity. Watching the film, you'd suspect that the word "Afrocentric" was conceived to describe it. Gerima, who labored to make *Sankofa* over a twenty-year period, had his film turned down by many indie distributors. I saw it in D.C., where the Howard University professor had gotten temporary use of a Cineplex Odeon managed by Ethiopians.

Sankofa was the kind of film no one in Hollywood would give a dime to make. Yet it is precisely the kind of film so many in the African-American community desire with all their hearts. When, in the last act, a slave girl kills a slave master who'd raped her repeatedly earlier in the story, the patrons stand up and cheer as if it were the climax of a Hollywood action movie. *Sankofa* didn't soft-peddle rape and slavery like, say, the miniseries *Queen*. Gerima's film was as hard and anti-white-supremacist as any film ever made involving black Americans. That much of the money for so stridently anti-colonial an enterprise came from Burkina Faso and other African countries is not surprising.

The question then arises: Who will see it? Dedicated filmmakers like Gerima will, come hell or high water, make their films. But what happens to them after they are made becomes a huge problem, especially when the film's message is as unpalatable to the mainstream as *Sankofa*'s. Gerima will show *Sankofa* at film festivals, colleges, and scattered commercial engagements. Without a distributor or financier to pay for additional prints, advertising, and promotion, *Sankofa* will most likely not reach its widest potential audience within the African-American community.

One long-term answer is the building of an African-American equivalent of the indie majors New Line or Miramax. Miramax, best known for skillfully marketing art films like *The Crying Game*, is now owned by Disney. But for most of its history, Miramax carefully cultivated the art-house crowd and became the industry's most consistently successful importer of foreign-language films. Miramax succeeded, and continues to, with niche marketing. Miramax's efforts to market African-American films (*A Rage in Harlem*, *Just Another Girl on the I.R.T.*) have been awkward, precisely because the company hasn't enough expertise in the area.

New Line, in contrast, has been quite smart in reaching young blacks. Every year they make one or two shots at reaching the active young black demographic. Their formula for profit has been hip-hop music, some rappers in the cast, and, most important, giving gifted young black filmmakers their first shot (e.g., the Hudlin brothers' *House Party*; the Hughes brothers' *Menace II Society*). The company's niche marketing has been so skillful that Ted Turner bought the company in order to pump more money into it, as Disney did with Miramax.

Both Miramax and New Line started small and through careful growth and intelligent production choices built into formidable companies. The black audiences exist to fill the role of a Miramax and a New Line. The "small budget + loving marketing + African-American subject = profit + increased market share + more work for black filmmakers" equation can work. A film with the guts of a *Sankofa* is just the kind of project such an institution can be built on.

But looking toward the twenty-first century, Miramax and New Line may already be obsolete models. The cost of making major motion pictures has always daunted anyone challenging Hollywood. It certainly is a big roadblock for the traditionally underfinanced black community. Perhaps the model to look at is the world of bootleg tapes and cassettes. Any major motion picture of interest to the black community is available before release in any swap meet, flea market, or sidewalk vendor in most urban areas. Even after a film like *CB4* is out and its video in the stores, these vendors still profit since the cost of the MCA home video (our initial list price was $93.69) is prohibitive compared to the $5 or $10 you pay in the neighborhood.

The development of a direct-to-home-video market for African-

American films will be crucial in any strategy to build a black film institution. The programming must be made as inexpensive and easily accessible as the bootlegs purchased by blacks. In fact, whoever starts this company might be well-advised to advertise their films as "legal bootlegs."

Cable was supposed to be the panacea for the control of the airwaves by a few monopolies. Of course, we now know that the big multinational corporations control cable and will likely set the speed limits on President Clinton's "information superhighway." Still, as the number of cable channels grows and the need for programming increases, there will be room for more than one black network. Already there are some black channels that, via satellite, broadcast black films. Robert Johnson, founder of Black Entertainment Television, has bought a pay-per-view channel and has announced his intention to do home video sales in conjunction with it. I'd be more excited about these moves if BET's management hadn't been so consistently conservative in its programming choices. Still, the general idea of a black cable network, able to commission films, show them on pay-per-view, and then sell them on home videos is, I think, an excellent one. And if the people behind BET don't execute this vision properly, I'm sure others will.

Financing is still, and will remain, a tricky issue for African-American cineastes. Everybody says they want more black films, but few feel secure enough to invest in them. It also raises the question, "If a black investor group puts together several million dollars, is starting a film distribution company the best way they can aid African-Americans?" As someone who loves film, I want to say "Yes" unequivocally. However, there are countless other ways such a group could helpfully invest that cash.

Let's say they do decide films are important enough to take the risk. Using either the New Line or pay-per-view model, "Bootleg Films" is inaugurated by black people. A good thing, indeed. But it is not the final answer either. Taking off my theoretical hat and putting on my practical cap, I know that filmmaking philosophy would be one of the biggest sticking points. As much as I admired *Sankofa* I know that many elements in the black community will be totally offended by its scathing critique of Christianity. Would Bootleg, despite its backing of Gerima's film, feel comfortable making

Menace II Society III, knowing it would make money even as it contradicted some of the messages of *Sankofa*? My reading of the conflicting moral strains running through the black community in the nineties tells me that there would be some bitter battles over that question.

So the answer isn't simply a cinematic Motown. It's a cinematic Motown and Nation of Islam, where the parables of the Honorable Elijah Muhammad are dramatized, and a cinematic Luke Records, where black pornography would be presented with a Miami-pumping bass in the background. Just as we need a diversity of black films we're going to need more than one brand of bootleg film. The Nation of Islam, with its sales of the *Final Call* newspaper, audiotapes, and other items via its membership, is actually only one or two steps removed from manifesting my theoretical black film distributor. All Minister Farrakhan needs is an ambitious young Black Muslim director, several hundred thousand from the Nation's savings, and a coupon in *The Final Call* to do it. That film is a guaranteed sales success, whether the Nation of Islam rents out a theater to display it or sells it directly on home video.

Similarly there is an emotionally rich, financially lucrative mother lode in the catalogue of unfilmed women's literature. *The Color Purple*, which I personally didn't like but which was embraced by women of all colors, didn't inspire a wave of novelistic adaptations but I'm confident that by the end of the century one of the most substantial wings of African-American cinema will be the filmed works of Toni Morrison, Terry McMillan, Ntosake Shange, Bebe Moore Campbell, etc. No question that this is a vital catalogue of great, very human stories waiting to be told.

Moreover, as book sales have testified, a national audience for the voices of black women clearly exists. The audiences have been consistently multiracial, though the works are steeped in the African-American experience. The strong ratings of the Oprah Winfrey–produced adaptation of Gloria Naylor's *The Women of Brewster Place*, along with the nearly $100 million gross of *Color Purple*, suggest to me there is a market that, perhaps, some ambitious black feminist producer may yet satisfy.

To be a twenty-first-century black is not to let the past chain you down. It is to see the future and rewrite it before it even starts.

Ultimately what I'm advocating is a downsizing of the African-American estimation of what the cinematic audience is and of the revenues these works generate. Like most Americans, we perceive film in mass terms. (Big budget + large audience = big check + wide celebrity.) The bootleg model I've described would directly serve target audiences within the African-American community. Then, depending on the movies' quality, these works could be sold to audiences beyond that target group.

To white indie filmmakers such as Hal Hartley or Jim Jarmusch, this discussion will likely sound naive. This is precisely how they've worked for years—making movies on a $2 budget and reaching out to arthouse audiences worldwide. On their terms, they're successful. My perception, however, is that the potential role of independent black cinema is still not appreciated by African-American audiences—or filmmakers. In addition, it runs contrary to the ambitions of a lot of filmmakers fixated on competing equally on the big-budget playing field of white Hollywood.

Perhaps my background in the areas of recording and publishing, two fields where smaller, more focused audiences are accepted and even desired, is what influences my thoughts. It strikes me that for black filmmakers to have the kind of steady, prolific, and profitable careers in features that an August Wilson's had in theater, a Toni Morrison in literature, or Luther Vandross in music, it can happen only with a mentality that leads away from the mass-market mania of Hollywood and the philosophical and economic restrictions that accompany it.

For example, there are a world of black bookstores and black publishers that are doing quite nicely because they supply black readers with texts that white publishers won't, at a reasonable price. These stores and writers aren't reinventing the wheel—they are just fulfilling the traditional role of communications in the black community: They speak directly to me of the things I need for sustenance and survival.

I know the equations won't be that simple. I understand that the complexities of personality, artistic aspirations, capital acquisition, and audience expectations all have an impact on the making and selling of any work in ways that can't be anticipated by rigid theories. Still, for me, my journey from the dingy Brooklyn theaters I attended as a child hasn't led me completely to Hollywood because there simply isn't enough room there for all the things I'm interested in. I find myself, time and again, drawn back to Brooklyn, to the streets where Spike Lee and Leslie Harris struggled, and to the theaters I recall from my childhood.

Sitting in those seats decades later, I still don't see on-screen the diversity of black faces I find in the streets. The difference is that now I do see a future in which, by making just a few steps (however financially risky), visual empowerment will be possible for people of color. My vision of twenty-first-century blacks is of people who know their history. But twenty-first-century blacks will not allow the frustration of the past to hold them down, to corrode their optimism or sense of fun. They will see the future and start rewriting it before it even begins. The technology's out there. So are the talent and the desire.

ACKNOWLEDGMENTS

I want to thank Thomas Cripps, Donald Bogle, the *Amsterdam News*'s Mel Tapley, Vicki Horsford, Spike Lee, John Pierson, Pam Gibson, Kevin Hooks, Mark Burg, Andre Harrell, John Singleton, Brian Grazer, Lisa Henson, Debbie Newmeyer, Meryl Poster, Bill Fay, Leslie Harris, and Erwin Wilson for the lessons in the history, business, and passion of moviemaking.

Special thanks to Reggie and Warrington Hudlin, Melissa Maxwell, Sean Daniel, Stephen Barnes, Bill Stephney, and Chris Rock for helping me enter the filmmaking fellowship.

In the book world, thanks to Wendy Wolf, Sarah Lazin, Wende Gozan, Eileen Campion, and Laura Nolan, and of course Von Alexander.

ACKNOWLEDGMENTS

INDEX

Nelson George is the author of eight nonfiction books on black culture, including *Where Did Our Love Go?*, *Elevating the Game*, *The Death of Rhythm & Blues*, and *Buppies, B-Boys, Baps & Bohos*. He has also written one novel, *Urban Romance*. He is a winner of the ASCAP-Deems Taylor Award and has been nominated for a National Book Critics Circle Award. A graduate of St. John's University, George was *Billboard*'s black music editor for seven years before becoming a regular columnist for *The Village Voice* in 1989. He has also written for *The New York Times* and many other national publications. He is the co-author of the films *Strictly Business* and *CB4*, for which he was also executive producer.

Nelson George was born and raised in Brooklyn, New York, where he still lives.